LEADERSHIP SUCCESS IN CHINA

An Expatriate's Guide

Yue-er Luo | Erik Duerring | William Byham | The DDI China Team

Published by DDI Press, c/o Development Dimensions International, World Headquarters—Pittsburgh, 1225 Washington Pike, Bridgeville, PA 15017-2838.

Manufactured in the United States of America.

Library of Congress Cataloging in Publications Data

Luo, Yue-er; Duerring, Erik; Byham, William; DDI China Team

Leadership success in China
An expatriate's guide
Yue-er Luo, Erik Duerring, William Byham, The DDI China Team

1. Business   2. Leadership   3. China

ISBN 978-0-9761514-4-9

10	9	8	7	6	5	4	3	2

DEDICATION

This book is dedicated to all those expatriate managers
who have shared their knowledge and experiences
and paved the way for others in China.

TABLE OF CONTENTS

INTRODUCTION

China's economic development today is phenomenal. As a manager and leader in China, you have the privilege of playing an active role in one of the most exciting transformations in recent world history. At a personal level your time leading and managing in China will be one of the most difficult, yet potentially rewarding, assignments you will ever have.

The complexities of managing a team steeped in a culture vastly different from your own should not be underestimated. And in the case of China, a cultural heritage that evolved over thousands of years lies at the heart of the challenge, compounded by 50 years of Communist rule.

You will find that some leadership and management techniques that apply in the West also work in China. But many do not. What works and what does not, along with advice on how your existing leadership and management skills will need to be augmented and modified to meet the China challenge, form the core of this book.

China comprises 33 province-level divisions, including 22 provinces, 5 autonomous regions, 4 municipalities, 2 special administrative regions, 56 ethnic groups, and more than 200 dialects. In terms of its ethnic and cultural diversity, China more closely resembles Europe than it does the United States. For example, Mandarin is the national language, but a 2007 survey estimated that only 53 percent of China's population can speak standard Mandarin[1]; the rest speak an assortment of regional dialects, many of which are mutually unintelligible. Chinese people also differ according to their age group and the differing political upheavals that have occurred during their lifetimes. These complexities mean that managing staff in China must be approached with great sensitivity and, above all, knowledge.

From the expatriate's point of view, not speaking Chinese adds yet another layer of complexity. But knowing the language as well as the natives won't necessarily reduce the cultural mismatch. Many expatriates who were born outside China but who are ethnically Chinese and who speak Mandarin—for example, many Hong Kong Chinese, the Taiwanese Chinese, or those who were born in mainland China but were educated abroad—can and frequently do come unglued by the cultural differences.

Expatriate managers need to contend with significant skill shortages too, particularly at the middle and top levels of management. The talent today tends to be first generation (born after the China economy opened up in 1980), and there are few role models for that generation. The parents of young, professional Chinese typically worked for state-owned companies that were concerned with production quotas and were indifferent to the needs of the market and the customer. Those Chinese who do have strong leadership and management skills are exceptional—and they're highly coveted. According to a 2007 research report by The Conference Board, finding qualified managerial talent rates as the greatest challenge of companies operating in Asia.[2]

No other country in the world has as many new companies entering the market annually as does China, and every new entrant is chasing local talent. A 2005 McKinsey study estimates that by 2010 China will require 75,000 top-level executives with global experience—about 70,000 more than the then-current number.[3] The scramble for staff will be one of your chief preoccupations. Keeping them will be another.

Opportunities abound in China; your dilemma is finding the right level of local talent so that you can chase those opportunities. In most cases you will lead a team that has far less experience than any other you have ever managed. The vast imbalance between the low talent supply and the high demand for it leads to many interrelated issues such as high employee turnover, rising employee expectations, and salary and title inflation. Your biggest problem will be finding enough local talent to meet all the expectations placed on you. It is the number one preoccupation of almost all expatriate managers in China, as found in research from Development Dimensions International (DDI). In 2006

DDI noted that 81 percent of a Chinese leadership survey's respondents said that their first priority was to improve or leverage their talent, compared with a significantly lower global figure of 66 percent found in 2005.[4]

Your task as an expatriate manager will not be easy, but your efforts will be worth it. You are in the right place at the right time to make a significant impact. China is a wonderfully interesting place for business managers because it is the fastest-growing area in the world. There is probably no better place to be an expatriate manager than in China. You will gain precious experience in leading a team of motivated, ambitious young individuals and working in a business environment in which speed and change are the norms. At a personal level, your time in China will be one of the most engaging and extraordinary experiences of your life. Professionally, the opportunity and challenges will give you the chance to shine; your career can be made in China! The purpose of this book is to help make that happen.

How This Book Is Organized

Chapter 1—Your Number One Problem: The Talent Shortage. Why are there too few talented local managers and leaders in China? China has many universities and millions graduate from them each year, so what are the problems? This chapter discusses the shortfall in the numbers and quality of local graduates and experienced middle managers relative to the demand. It also examines the implications of the shortfall: high employee turnover, title inflation, and salary escalation.

Chapter 2—The Chinese Employee. China's population is diverse; as a result, there is no single, defining model of the Chinese employee. This chapter looks at some common characteristics that most mainland Chinese share and then examines the age variations and each age group's differing experiences caused by China's recent political upheavals. The management and leadership challenges that arise from these differences are then assessed.

Chapter 3—Attracting Qualified Applicants. Companies compete fiercely to acquire qualified graduates in China. How to attract them is the subject of this chapter. Well-known multinationals with excellent reputations have little trouble in attracting good applicants, but how do lesser-known or new entrants to the China market make themselves appealing to desirable job seekers? What are these applicants looking for? And what turns them off?

Chapter 4—Selecting Your Team. Once you have acquired a strong field of applicants, how do you choose among them in the China context? This chapter looks at the hiring traps in China and the strategies you can use to avoid them.

Chapter 5—The Essential Nature of Trust. Perhaps the singularly most-defining characteristic of all relationships in China is trust. You will achieve very little with your China team if trust is absent. It takes time to establish, it's easy to lose, and once lost, it's difficult to regain. Even when you have lost it, that fact may not be immediately apparent. This chapter examines the trust traps that lurk in the Chinese workplace and strategies to avoid them and to enhance trust.

Chapter 6—Setting the Direction for Your China Team. Chinese culture demands strong, decisive leadership. You must lay out a vision for your team—one in which each member can see his or her place. This will garner trust and respect and help with retaining your staff. But how do you do this and get your team to buy in? This chapter explains how.

Chapter 7—Getting Your Team to Act Like a Team. Younger Chinese have little experience at being "team players." One of your tasks as a leader will be to forge your young, ambitious reports into a cooperating, communicating, and cohesive team. Cultural factors will make this much harder than you expect. This chapter outlines a plan to achieve this goal.

Chapter 8—Training Your Employees. Training is essential in China. Your Chinese staff will need to gain many more skills so that they can work effectively in your international organization and improve their cultural fit within it. But also in China—perhaps more than anywhere else—training serves as a key retention driver for your staff. How training should be delivered and how it can be leveraged are the subjects of this chapter.

Chapter 9—Coaching Your Team. Coaching complements training, and it represents one of the main methods by which people learn on the job. The dearth of managerial talent in China means that your role as a coach will never be more important. How you coach also depends on whether your local reports are younger or older. This chapter examines what conventional coaching techniques can be used in China and how they should be modified for China's unique conditions.

Chapter 10—Managing Your Team's Performance. Managing a team's performance represents many managers' least preferred task. But in China, performance management is even more difficult. This chapter explains why and offers a series of strategies aimed at overcoming the difficulties and getting your local staff more accustomed to accepting accountability.

Chapter 11—Growing Ready Local Leaders. Recruiting local senior leaders and managers often is not an option in China. At this stage in China's economic development, there simply are too few. So many organizations have no option other than to develop their own pool of leaders. This chapter provides valuable advice on how to do this in China.

Chapter 12—Keeping Your Team. Personnel poaching is rampant in China. The chances are that your best local reports will be tagged by headhunters. What makes people susceptible to outside offers? Is it simply a matter of money, or are other factors important? This chapter examines what you can do to keep your team.

Chapter 13—Getting Off to a Fast Start. An expatriate assignment in China requires plenty of predeparture preparation and a well-conceived plan for the first few months after your arrival. This chapter provides advice on what to do, based on the experiences of other expatriates who have held China assignments.

CHAPTER 1

Your Number One Problem: The Talent Shortage

The Supply Side: Quantity and Quality of Graduates in China[1]

Quantity Issues

China is committed to upgrading its universities, but there are two problems:

- The state university sector can barely keep up with demand.
- The types of courses they emphasize tend to be in the sciences and technology.

China claims to have at least 17 million university students, but that's out of a population of 1.3 billion people. (The United States has roughly the same number of college students from a population of 390 million.) But it's not just a matter of quantity.

Even though the Chinese government now spends more on education than ever before, that spending has not kept pace with economic growth. Education spending has been almost static in proportion to the total economy. A 1993 target to spend 4 percent of the gross domestic product (GDP) on education by 2000 remained unmet even in 2007, so the goal was shifted. The government now hopes to meet that 4 percent figure by 2010.[2]

A 1986 local government requirement that all children receive at least nine years of education was not combined with an adequate funding increase; as a result, China missed this target as well. Nor have funding increases been adequate to meet the more than threefold increase in the number of tertiary students since 1999. The dilemma will only grow. There are around 17 million tertiary students today; by 2010, there will be approximately 25 million.

Quality Issues

Quality is another problem. The government has placed little or no emphasis on the liberal arts and related disciplines, which require critical thinking about politics, economics, and society. In 2007 only 32 percent of China's university population was enrolled in arts and humanities, and of this number 20 percent was enrolled in languages.[3] But creativity, questioning minds, and an aptitude for risk taking are what China most lacks among its graduates and what multinational companies most complain about as missing in their China employees.

China's education system does not emphasize application, and rarely do students take on team project work. Instead, the primary mode of learning is memorization and rote. Students get a strong theoretical background, but relatively little opportunity or encouragement to be innovative and creative by putting their learning into practice. Universities are ranked by examination results only. And while a graduate might come from a highly ranked university, his or her degree provides little indication of capability for mastering work complexity in the real world. What it does tend to mean is that the graduates are strong in theoretical work yet weak in application and, above all, are highly skilled at passing exams.

According to one educator who has taught in China, "The importance of liberal arts also includes the ability to think 'laterally.' I find that most graduates from local schools have a very low tolerance for ambiguity in business discussions. It is the rare individual who takes a truly bold stand and/or leap of faith when solving a company's problems. Most prefer the comfort of saying 'there's not enough data or information to make an informed decision.' This presents a genuinely global challenge for Chinese companies that are competing against Western organizations populated by more expansive thinkers. While Chinese managers might be capable implementers, far fewer are innovative strategists. It is the ability to extrapolate trends and derive meaning that leads to true value from the trends' implications."[4]

So, rather than establishing programs that engender creative thinking, China is pouring money into creating world-class university laboratories and attracting top-level science and technology academic staff from abroad. It is important that China does this, but it is still only half of what is required to provide a full university curriculum in a Western sense.

China's government intrudes in research like nowhere else. Not a single university in China has the freedom of expression and inquiry that is routine among top universities in the U.S., the U.K., or Australia. As a result, China's higher-learning institutions turn out students who are good at following orders rather than being creative. Graduates are competent rather than clever.

"Right now, I don't think any university in China has an atmosphere comparable to the older Western universities—Harvard or Oxford—in terms of freedom of expression," Lin Jianhua, the executive vice president of Peking University, has said.[5]

Few universities in China are comparable in quality to universities in Europe or the U.S.—even when it comes to the sciences and technology. A handful of top institutions sit at the pinnacle of the pyramid, and then there are the rest—the distance between them is immense. This difference in quality means that raw numbers are misleading. Gary Gereffi and Vivek Wadha at Duke University were intrigued by the commonly repeated assertion that only 70,000 engineers graduate from U.S. universities each year while China produces 600,000 engineering graduates and India 350,000.[6] When they took a closer look at the numbers and compared like with like, they found that the numbers of graduates from rigorous, four-year, engineering-degree programs rose to 137,000 for the U.S., but fell to 112,000 in India and 351,000 in China. The Chinese figures probably still represent an exaggeration because a large number of so-called "engineering graduates" are more the caliber of car mechanics.[7]

In another study the McKinsey Global Institute conducted interviews with 83 HR professionals involved with hiring local graduates in low-wage countries and found that between 2003 and 2008 China would produce 15.7 million graduates. Of these, only 1.2 million—fewer than 10 percent—would be suitable to work for a multinational employer in the nine occupations studied: engineers, life science researchers, finance workers, accountants, generalists, quantitative analysts, doctors, nurses, and support staff. The figure for India was far higher—about 25 percent—but still low in absolute terms.[8]

Another problem is that the graduates are not always where the (multinational) jobs are. According to the McKinsey report, just one quarter of all Chinese graduates live in a city or region close to a major international airport—a requirement of most multinationals setting up offshore facilities. And only one-third of all Chinese graduates are willing to relocate to other provinces for work.

The Supply Side: Too Few Talented, Experienced Middle Managers

DDI's 2005 *Leadership in China* survey asked HR professionals and leaders to select the top 10 most critical skills for leaders from a set of 22 possible skills. Survey results revealed that Chinese leaders view motivating others, building trust, retaining talent, and leading high-performance teams as the most highly valued skills. But the survey also showed that almost a quarter of Chinese managers are weak in these skills.[9] All too often, China's growth has forced organizations to place too many potentially good candidates into management roles too early.

Other factors have contributed to the acute shortage of mid-level management and leadership talent. The low birth rate, caused by the nationwide famine of 1959–1961 and the one-child policy, is a factor, as is the Cultural Revolution of 1967–1976, which disrupted education and work opportunities for those who are now age 50–60. The ongoing "brain drain" brought on by many young, talented Chinese leaving their home country—never to return—is yet another factor.

Might the answer be found in China's business schools? Most likely, no. Business schools have problems similar to the undergraduate schools.[10] The Chinese Ministry of Education (MOE) first licensed schools to grant MBAs in 1991, beginning with 9 universities with 100 students. By 2001 the MOE had approved 62 institutions with 10,000 students enrolled. But after the top group of about 13 business schools came a stream of other institutions offering credentials rather than education. Often, courses are taught by poorly trained faculty. Not surprisingly, they churn out graduates with no discernible skills. Other schools are little more than "diploma mills" that provide credentials for a fee, but precious little education.[11] Despite the enrollment explosion in Chinese business schools, most corporate recruiters give graduates poor to middling marks, according to a *Business Week* survey of more than 170 corporate recruiters at both Chinese and multinational companies in China.[12]

Many Chinese universities formed partnerships with U.S, Australian, European, and Hong Kong schools to offer better-quality, state-approved MBA programs. The elite Chinese universities, such as Peking and Tsinghua Universities in Beijing and Fudan University in Shanghai, have forged strong links with top U.S. schools. Massachusetts Institute of Technology (MIT) has an MBA program at Tsinghua, and many of its faculty have each spent six months at the Sloan School; others have spent time at Harvard. Fudan has been sending faculty to MIT for the last 10 years. Through these partnerships the Chinese aim to create a super league of universities that can produce graduates of the right caliber. But even these top graduates can lack adequate English skills and problem-solving abilities. The problem links back to the poor system of elementary and secondary education. After all, the universities can work with only what they have been given.

Some multinational companies, including ABN AMRO, Bayer, Citigroup, Alcatel-Lucent, and Philips, have decided to take matters into their own hands and have become big donors to Chinese business schools. This influx of financial support helps to improve the education that can be offered and gives the donor companies an option to be the first to review the best of the new graduates.

An additional problem has arisen in recent years: To tap a source of extra funds, some of China's better higher-education institutions have franchised their names to sister institutions that charge high fees. The quality of these institutions is questionable and often not on a par with the parent institution. To some extent, they are fee-generating organizations more than educational institutions. Hiring managers need to discern whether an applicant's qualifications are from the prestigious university or merely from one that has been set up to imitate it.

Yet another dilemma is that some institutions are entirely bogus or grossly misrepresent themselves and their capabilities. Some offer nothing more than a web site. One such institution, registered to a Beijing residential address, tried to mimic INSEAD, one of Europe's top business schools. The institution's web site went so far as to include photographs of actual INSEAD faculty, suggesting that the two schools were somehow linked.[13] Essentially, this institution had parasitically assumed the characteristics of INSEAD in the hope of fooling potential students and their prospective employers into thinking that it worked in tandem with INSEAD.

The massive exodus from China of promising students who attend universities abroad and then decide not to return to their home country is another significant concern. Research by the Chinese Academy of Social Sciences suggests that of the approximately one million young Chinese who have studied abroad since the 1980s, approximately two-thirds chose to stay overseas after graduation. Since 2002 more than 100,000 students have gone abroad to study each year, but the number of returnees hovers between 20,000 and 30,000.[14]

The Demand Side: High Demand for Mid-Level Managers and Professionals

When asked about their challenges in building the local business, CEOs in China consistently cite "people" as their biggest obstacle. A 2006 survey of U.S. companies by the American Chamber of Commerce in Shanghai found that the talent shortage had overtaken bureaucracy as the top headache for U.S. companies in China.[15] Jeff Barnes, chief learning officer at General Electric (GE) in China, said that the "issue we have is finding mid-level and top-level leadership."[16]

Increasingly, multinational companies must compete for staff with local companies that are growing in their dynamism and agility.[17] The Shanghai Automotive Industry Corporation (SAIC), Lenovo, Haier, Huawei, and China State Construction International are among the Chinese companies that have begun to compete internationally. They too now draw on the same pool of graduates as multinationals in China. They have joined the poaching game and now attempt to recruit mid-level and senior Chinese managers from foreign companies.

Human Resource Implications

China's talent shortfall gives rise to a number of human resource considerations. They might be common to most developing, but fast-growing, economies; but in China, their scale and intensity carry an exponential impact.

Employee Turnover

With the paucity of good local managers and leaders in China, turnover is high and poaching is rife. Getting good staff is only half the battle; the other half is keeping them.

In 2007 employee turnover at multinational companies in China was estimated to be 14.3 percent.[18] Employees are even more mobile in large coastal cities. For example, in bustling Shanghai and Guangdong province, some companies lose a third of their employees every year.[19] Turnover at state-owned enterprises is far lower. Their employees tend to have fewer marketable skills or to not want to lose their welfare benefits, such as subsidized housing loans or company-provided housing. In 2006 the highest turnover rates of non-manual workers were in sales (19.8 percent) and marketing (18.5 percent) in Beijing.[20]

Premature Promotion and Title Inflation

One tactic companies use to keep promising young staff is to promote them. Unfortunately, those promoted often aren't ready for significant leadership and management positions. Another commonly employed retention tactic is to give employees a loftier title but without a commensurate increase in responsibilities. Although this can help increase retention, it does lead to title inflation.

Expatriates soon learn that in China a job title generally provides a poor indication of an individual's abilities. Title inflation can make a company's leadership team appear full and strong on paper when, in fact, the reality can be very different. Another side effect of this phenomenon is that Chinese employees begin to overestimate their own abilities and develop a sense of false entitlement.

Salary Escalation

Salaries for capable local staff can rise substantially each year. Hewitt Consulting found that annual salary increases for all categories of staff averaged 8.8 percent for 2007, and it estimates this figure to be 8.7 percent for 2008. Mid-level management received the highest salary increases among all categories of staff, averaging 10.3 percent in 2007.[21]

Even with these increases, the expectations of the young, ambitious talent in the booming markets are incredible. In the same 2007 compensation survey, Hewitt pointed out that only 28 percent of Chinese employees think they are paid enough relative to their performance and contribution.[22] Another report from an HR consulting firm confirmed a similar upward salary trend, forecasting a salary increase for white-collar staff in all industries to be 8.4 percent in 2008.[23]

But having said that, salaries for professionals in China are not high relative to what talented local professionals earn in other business cities—for instance, they are about one-third to one-half of their U.S. counterparts.[24] But pay is rising. According to a senior partner at Korn/Ferry International, Chinese leaders with strong track records could expect a 10–20 percent salary increase in 2007.[25] Rule changes at Hong Kong's stock exchange in 2006 required for the first time that Chinese companies listed in Hong Kong disclose the remuneration of their senior office holders. And thus it was disclosed that Guo Shuqing, the chairman of China Construction Bank, one of China's biggest banks, was paid US$107,000 in 2005.[26] His U.S. equivalent would receive 50–100 times that salary. Guo's example is not unusual in China.

To prevent poaching, many Japanese and Western employers in China now write penalty clauses into the contracts of locally recruited engineers, stipulating that if they leave within a predetermined period, they must repay a portion of their salary to cover training costs. However, this threat is often nullified by other employers who are more than ready to pay the fee for the engineers they want to recruit. Furthermore, provisions that seek to bind employees to particular employers might contravene International Labor Organization (ILO) conventions against bonded labor, where they are relevant. The China Labor Law, passed in 2007 and to be implemented in 2008, also prohibits such bonding.[27]

But then, not all companies in China experience high turnover. One recent survey found that Spansion (China) Ltd., Four Seasons Hotel Shanghai, Shanghai Johnson Co. Limited, Three on the Bund, and Federal Express all reported losing fewer than 10 percent of their new recruits in the first year compared with 17 percent for all foreign companies surveyed, and 9 percent in the second year compared with 17 percent.[28] While conditions in China make retention very difficult, there remains an element of choice. What helps a company to keep its staff in China is explored later in this book.

China's economic development is going full speed ahead. The demand for skilled professional employees and good managers will continue to escalate in the short and medium terms. If current growth rates continue, then the problem will worsen before it improves. Inevitably, expatriate managers will be forced to spend more time on people issues than anything else. It is an unavoidable reality and something for which every expatriate manager needs to be prepared mentally and in terms of their skill capabilities as they arrive in China to take up their assignment.

CHAPTER 2

The Chinese Employee

What is the profile of a typical Chinese employee? What sets the Chinese worker apart from employees you are accustomed to working with in the West? Because China is so diverse in terms of its dialects and accents, regional nuances, and demographics, there is always the risk of oversimplifying the answers to these important questions. But there are ways of thinking and doing things that are common to most local employees in China, who are fundamentally shaped by one or a mixture of three different cultural layers:

- First and foremost, your employees in China are in every aspect Chinese. Most likely, they have grown up and been educated in an environment that is only Chinese.

- Second, they will be influenced by a national culture that was strictly Marxist/Maoist at least until 1980. But traditional Chinese values have changed since this time, such as ideas about the appropriate role for women.

- The third significant layer of influence relates to the period in which individuals grew up. China's modern history has been marked by far-reaching upheavals, with the Cultural Revolution being the most recent. It has had a very direct impact on people's lives—how they think and how they behave at work.

What are the main characteristics of each of these three layers?

Chinese, First and Foremost

Many nuances and subtleties combine to make someone mainland Chinese, but five elements are critical:

- An indirect communication style
- The need to save face
- Respect for age and authority
- Strong family values
- A strong preference to follow the leader

Indirect Communication Style

It is not uncommon for newly arrived expatriates to find themselves shaking their heads after a conversation with their Chinese employees, wondering what was the discussion's purpose. People in China tend to be indirect in all communication, be it spoken or written. This is particularly so when they are praising or disagreeing with each other; they usually don't give details about the praise or why they disagree. Instead, they talk in generalities. It becomes important, then, to read between the lines and to understand the context of the message to glean its real meaning. Targeted questions with in-depth follow-up also can be asked privately or outside a meeting situation to ascertain the real message. But all the while, people avoid confrontation or directly addressing one another unless they actually mean to cause discomfort or insult.

The Chinese approach business discussions in the same indirect manner. They start from a general point where agreement is assured, postponing the details for a later time or another meeting when they can add content and context in the course of working out an agreement. This is almost the reverse of the way business is done in the West, where details must be nailed down and agreements specified before any documents are signed. These differences in thinking are the source of many misunderstandings, both in business and personal interactions. The key to success for the expatriate is to recognize and respect these differences, while finding a way to work around them to everyone's benefit.

Need to Save Face

In China, when people have a different point of view in meetings and discussions with others, they tend to give only subtle hints that they disagree. They will not directly say they have another opinion. Their desire to maintain harmony and mutual respect drives the behaviors of "giving and saving face"; no one is ever told they're wrong in public or in front of others unless the deliberate intention is to humiliate them. Similarly, rarely do you hear a flat "no" in China. Instead, less-direct forms of disagreement are used, such as "It may not be possible" or "I will try my best." The Chinese thus look for nonverbal clues when communicating with each other so that they receive the entire message rather than the ambiguous, partial message—that which is spoken.

Individuals often prefer to agree with others in order to remain in their good graces and to avoid risking the relationship by voicing what they really think. The importance of personal relationships (and the need to preserve face for self and others) over business relationships leads people to avoid taking a stand or action that may go against what others think. Or, they might avoid taking corrective action if it means causing offense or losing face.

This concern for saving face also means that individuals often perceive asking for help as a sign of incompetence or weakness. In the workplace, for example, when an individual avoids sharing a problem or issue with a manager, it might well be due to a desire to save face rather than a lack of willingness to accept responsibility or ownership of a task or problem.

Respect for Age and Authority

Age, rank, and authority are highly interrelated in mainland Chinese culture. Age does not guarantee an individual authority as the formal or informal leader of a group, but it helps. On the other hand, young people typically do not lead teams or groups. Such leaders tend to be well into their forties or older.

Group leaders who are not the oldest will take care to give face to older team members. This does not reduce the leaders' authority; rather, it enhances it because they are observing social norms and doing what is believed to be right. These younger leaders also must build credibility with their people by demonstrating their special skills or qualifications.

Strong Family Values

China's culture exudes a strong sense of family and family values. These values are stronger than in most Western cultures and extend far beyond having family gatherings at Chinese festivals or taking care of aging parents. The Chinese family values are reflected in filial piety, as children take their parents' views on personal decisions such as marriage, career choices, jobs, etc. Similarly, a person who succeeds in his or her career will publicly tell others, "I make my parents proud of me because of my achievement."

Strong ties between brothers and sisters can be demonstrated in the form of financial support for education or other financial assistance.

Strong Preference to Follow the Leader

In China respect and loyalty for authority are held in high regard. And loyalty to a leader is demonstrated by following the leader. The leader–follower relationship is modeled on parental relationships. The followers expect the leader to have regard for them almost like a guardian or parent would regard children in a family setting.

Once leadership is established, there is a much stronger relationship between the leader and his or her team than is typically seen in Western countries. Leadership also attaches to people rather than positions; for example, a retired leader is still highly respected in China. And leaders are expected to show interest in the personal well being of their team members. They must understand their employees not only in the work context, but also on a personal level. This is required of all workplace managers, whether they are local or expatriate. The paternalistic relationship extends to how employees expect to be remunerated. Housing, transportation, and health care expenses often are covered by the employer in state enterprises and, to some extent, in many private Chinese and multinational firms.

Such characteristics lead to very different behaviors and preferences in the workplace compared with the norm in, say, the U.S., European, or Australian workplace. And so there may be a mismatch of preferences and expectations between the typical Chinese employee and the Western expatriate manager who is more accustomed to managing Western staff at home. Table 2.1 summarizes some of the differences between typical Chinese and Western employees.

TABLE 2.1: Some Differences Between Chinese and Western Employees[1]

A Typical Local Chinese Employee . . .	A Typical Western Employee . . .
Prefers strict orders to follow.	Views strict orders as insulting and an affront to personal integrity.
Considers a job done well if the right processes have been followed.	Is results driven; a job is done well if the desired goals have been met.
Prefers lots of supervision.	Prefers little supervision.
Prefers little or no performance pay.	Prefers productivity-related bonuses.
Does not like to speak up in meetings.	Views meetings as a community to exchange thoughts and ideas.
Would rather resign than express a grievance.	Is quick to express grievances.
Prefers clear-cut situations—they reduce anxiety caused by risk.	Is able to navigate ambiguity and make judgments.
Views the employer/manager as a "father."	Views the employer/manager as a colleague.
Is able to operate with only partial knowledge about the company.	Prefers to be privy to everything about the company.
Accepts boredom in the workplace if it's a consequence of following orders from leaders.	Often would rather resign than be bored.
Views orders as commands to be adhered to.	Views orders as suggestions to be modified and improved upon.
Prefers not to accept risk.	Can accept and work with risk.

The Impact of Communism

Mainland Chinese culture has been influenced by an additional dimension: Communist rule and the closed-door policy of the 1950s through the 1970s that isolated China and left it without the benefit of significant outside influences. This affected the mainland culture in a way that Chinese culture in, say, Taiwan or Hong Kong was not. It meant that the mainland Chinese would behave and think differently than Chinese elsewhere in the world. The following pages examine how Communism has left its indelible mark on mainland Chinese and what it means for you as a leader.

Employer Paternalism Endures

Chairman Mao Zedong introduced the "iron rice bowl" policy, whereby all workers were assigned to a work unit that not only provided them with lifelong employment, but also maintained cradle-to-grave responsibility for each worker and his or her family. Elements of this mentality endure to this day. Social Security payments as a proportion of salaries that employers in China must pay are among the highest in Asia. For example, in Shanghai a company turns over 44 percent of each employee's base salary[2] to the government as a Social Security payment, which is supposed to cover basic health and pension provisions. As mentioned, employees in China expect their company to pay for additional medical benefits, housing, insurance, transportation, and meals. These kinds of benefits are usually paid on an equal basis; that is, everyone is entitled to the same amount regardless of their contribution or value to the company. Nonetheless, change has come. Economic progress has reduced job security and eroded old certainties. The expectation of paternalistic care and remuneration remains, but it is waning.

Scarce-Resources Mentality

China has been through many periods of upheaval, social dislocation, and poverty. Civil war and then the Cultural Revolution brought great hardships. Consequently, mainland Chinese culture has evolved with a scarce-resources mentality. There is a "zero-sum" view of the world, based on a perception that resources are fixed; therefore, personal advancement can come only at the expense of someone else. Of course, with the rapid economic growth that China enjoys today, this is not happening—the pie is growing all the time—but such thinking remains ingrained. This mentality has both a positive and a negative impact. On the plus side, it helps to make many young Chinese ambitious employees; the downside is that it drives people to win at the expense of others.

Overly Competitive and Unwilling to Share

Such a scarce-resource mentality induces many in the Chinese workplace to be competitive in a negative sense and less willing to share. This behavior includes hoarding resources rather than sharing them—even with members of the same team. Also, knowledge, information, useful networking, or key contacts that can aid in accomplishing team goals might be held back. Individuals might think that providing or sharing with the rest of the team will limit their chances for personal success. With this mind-set employees might be part of a team, but exhibit little, if any, team spirit.

The Cultural Revolution's Role in Creating Age-Related Layers of Talent

Figure 2.1 segments China's population by age and gender. It also links age to momentous events in China's recent history, such as the Cultural Revolution, which had an extraordinary impact on shaping the culture of that generation.

Figure 2.1: Mainland Chinese Population by Gender and Age[3]

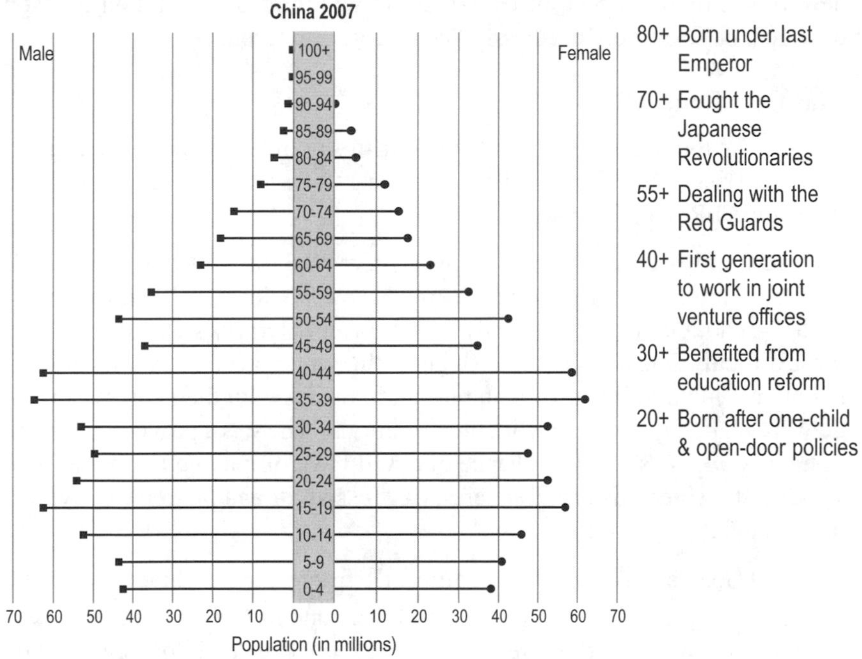

China 2007

80+	Born under last Emperor
70+	Fought the Japanese Revolutionaries
55+	Dealing with the Red Guards
40+	First generation to work in joint venture offices
30+	Benefited from education reform
20+	Born after one-child & open-door policies

Male / Female — age bands from 100+ down to 0-4

Population (in millions): 70 60 50 40 30 20 10 0 0 10 20 30 40 50 60 70

Source: U.S. Census Bureau, International Data Base

Officially, the Cultural Revolution lasted from 1967 to 1976, but its impact has endured. Those who experienced its privations and hardships are distinctly different from other age groups. The Cultural Revolution had a profound impact on China's education system. Many schools were closed, while formal university education simply ceased to exist from 1967 to 1976. Universities were replaced by the "country movement," whereby people were "rusticated"—sent to work in villages across China to "learn" from the peasants. Universities only restarted in the mid-1970s.

One cannot overstate the dislocation caused by the Cultural Revolution—its effects are still evident today in the enormous disparities in education between generations. There are those who were directly affected (the "Lost Generation"); those who suffered partly or indirectly (the "In-Betweeners"); and today's young (the "Young, Hungry Tigers"), who received a formal education that was probably far superior to that of their parents. Because of this, there is not the blind reverence to Mao's memory in China that newcomers might expect; instead, there is widespread recognition that some of Mao's policies were needlessly destructive and wrong.

The Lost Generation

People who today are in their mid to late fifties or older sometimes are referred to as the Lost Generation because of the years of education they missed when the Cultural Revolution was in full swing.

As a result, this group is weak in basic literacy skills. Their learning ability also was impaired—they never learned how to learn. Members of this group—who are employed mostly in state-run enterprises—tend to have the most difficult time adapting to change in the workplace. Also, they prefer to maintain a low profile at work and in relationships with their supervisors, and they are relatively less open with their opinions. There is a proverb in Chinese: "The less one says, the less chance one will have of making a mistake." It is an adage to which this group adheres. If pressed for an opinion, they typically offer one that is neutral.

The Lost Generation also differs significantly from younger Chinese in that they:
- Have a higher level of respect for authority and hierarchy, both at work and with the government. Therefore, they are more keen to follow organizational policy and practices.
- Have a higher level of loyalty to company leaders.
- Are less willing to let go of old ideals, philosophies, and values.
- Have a higher tolerance for hardship and show greater persistence.
- Tend to observe from and remain on the sidelines before they will step up to volunteer for a change or transition.
- Have a low level of trust toward others until they have seen that they can be trusted.

The Cultural Revolution was a deeply disturbing time for China. Many Chinese remain hurt and scarred emotionally and mentally by what they had to endure during this period. Few want to talk openly about their experiences. Suffice to say, the upheavals and humiliations created feelings of insecurity, and many who lived through this period remain untrusting and cautious. The lack of trust contributes to an inhibition to confront problems openly.

But at a personal level, many of the Lost Generation have made a significant effort to try to catch up on the education that they missed. The group is now reaching retirement age—some have been given "compulsory" early retirement as loss-making, state-owned organizations have been closed, sold off, or merged.

From the Lost Generation, but Finding His Way in Today's China

Chen Jun is in his early fifties. His education was interrupted by the Cultural Revolution, but he managed to earn an engineering degree from Harbin University of Science and Technology after the universities reopened in the late 1970s.

Chen was 15 years old when the Cultural Revolution started in 1967. He grew up in a small town in the Tianjin area, but at the onset of the Revolution was sent to boarding school in the cold, remote northeast of China. It was an experience that helped Chen develop a strong, resilient character.

He is now the general manager of a gas-supply company in a medium-sized northern city that has a large number of small to medium-sized industries that use his company's product. Chen joined the company five years ago when it was acquired by a Hong Kong corporation. Thanks in large part to his good relationships with important people in the city's business and government circles who recommended him, Chen was recruited by the new investors to represent their interests. Although he did not have Western management experience or exposure, Chen's new employers felt that, given the sector and its reliance on government relationships, his connections and knowledge of the local bureaucracy outweighed what he lacked.

Chen has a low-key, gentle style. He represents well the interests of the original managers without offending the Hong Kong joint venture (JV) partners. Chen is sensitive to others and adept at playing a middleman role between the partners. The joint venture is profitable, and the partners cooperate well, thanks in large part to Chen.

Chen is satisfied with his current level of contribution. He is modest and maintains a low profile in keeping with his traditional Chinese heritage. He talks softly and prefers not to stand out as is more the norm in the Western executive world. When his boss, the president of the Hong Kong company, asked whether he wished to step up to the role of regional general manager responsible for several JVs in central China, Chen indirectly declined. Chen believes that being a regional manager would stretch his capabilities too far, partly because the position requires managing several managers from outside China.

Chen feels that he is already much more "progressive" than his Lost Generation peers, who mostly prefer to remain in their comfort zones. Given his background, Chen has achieved a great deal, but he feels that there are limits.

The In-Betweeners

This group comprises Chinese in their forties and early fifties—people who were somewhat affected by the Cultural Revolution, but who benefited from the opportunities created by the opening of China during the '80s. People in this group share characteristics with both the new generation—the Young, Hungry Tigers—and those of the conservative, quiet Lost Generation.

The In-Betweeners were the first to be significantly exposed to the Western culture that arrived with the inflow of investment from multinational companies and the establishment of joint ventures in the '80s. They are eager to learn from the West, but remain essentially mainland Chinese in culture. Successful members of this group are often particularly tenacious. In-Betweeners are typically proud of their ambition and tenacity. They think they are much stronger because when they were young, the universities were closed, and they were sent to rural areas to learn from the peasants. Having faced this type of hardship at an early age, In-Betweeners believe they can bite any bullet and are much tougher than the young generation, which has had an easier path growing up.

Profile of an In-Betweener

Liu Qiang is the CEO of a private company that makes industrial equipment in a relatively remote inner city in China. He is 46 years old and graduated from university in 1981. Liu was part of the first group of graduates who experienced the post-Cultural Revolution reforms of 1977. But the Cultural Revolution did have an adverse effect on his high school education—he missed learning many of the foundational skills that are usually taught in high school, although he acquired many of these skills through self-study.

After his university education Liu started his career as an engineer in an equipment company. The company was "privatized" in 1985, meaning it would no longer be funded by the government and was responsible for its own profits and losses. Liu was one of the few in the company to have a good education and was handpicked by the CEO and groomed to be his successor. Liu was promoted to CEO in 2000.

As CEO and leader, Liu is respected and well regarded because of his technical expertise, education, and management style. An enthusiastic learner, he enrolled in an 18-month, part-time EMBA program at a reputable private graduate school in Beijing. Each month he travels there for a long weekend of classes. The EMBA program requires at least four days of full-time study per month and another 30 to 40 hours of reading and studying.

Liu is seen as a progressive leader, while being sensitive to and appreciative of the company's heritage. He is bold in trying Western management concepts and tools, but he introduces them cautiously.

He has six direct reports in vice-president positions, four of whom are more than 10 years older than he is. They have much less management and technical expertise than he does. Under the coaching of the previous CEO, Liu has learned how to manage and work closely with this group of senior executives. When he has plans for driving a new policy or change, he first seeks the views of this group. Liu is patient and listens well. He also spends time strategizing how to win over his managers and other staff by creating practical incentives for change.

Liu also is intellectually sharp. Although he is quick at pinpointing the heart of both technical and management problems, he waits for the right time to share his opinions in order to save face for his colleagues. Liu is clear about the changes he wants to make to keep his company outperforming its competitors. However, he is well aware that at least 30 percent of his employees belong to the Lost Generation. They have relatively low skills, but are hard working and loyal. Liu works out his change strategies in progressive moves so that everyone can see and feel the benefits of change and have time to adjust.

The Young, Hungry Tigers

Those under 40 years old in China today comprise the Young, Hungry Tigers category. Born in the late 1970s after the Cultural Revolution, they were unaffected by the university and school closures.

This group is more exposed to information, Western culture, products, and know-how than any preceding generation. They are the group most sought after by multinational employers—as professional team members and as young managers. They are much easier to mold to a company's culture. However, they tend to overestimate their own ability and feel the job expectations that were established for previous generations are set too low for them. The Tigers also are very Internet savvy—the World Wide Web has become their main source of information and their window to the rest of the world.

What are the Tigers' other characteristics? They want to get rich quickly, even at the expense of others. They are increasingly nationalistic. Nationalism has replaced Communism as China's state ideology; while many are interested in the West, they also tend to be very pro-China. And Young, Hungry Tigers are tenacious—many must overcome extraordinary odds to get where they want to be. Examples abound, such as the engineering director of a large construction company. Now in his mid thirties, he grew up in remote Hebei Province in a village that did not have electricity. His fascination with something that he was unable to take for granted—electricity—saw him complete a degree in electrical engineering at university.

A Young, Hungry Tiger Has Trouble Leading

Vincent Zhang started high school in 1980, after the schools reopened in the wake of the Cultural Revolution. Because Vincent was able to attend high school uninterrupted, his basic skills are much better than those only a few years older.

Vincent studied electrical engineering at university and, after graduation in 1990, joined a foreign company as a software engineer. He did not consider Chinese companies after graduation, because he felt he could learn more at a foreign company. His English and other basic skills gave him the confidence and capability he needed to work there.

At 39, Vincent is now the local director of technology at a global IT company that views China as a strategic market and a source for R&D. This is Vincent's fourth employer since graduation. He has been with this organization for five years, during which time he has been promoted once from manager to director. He is perceived as a local with strong management potential. But Vincent is open to a job move if it will give him new challenges and responsibilities. He feels that he is ready to go to the next level.

Vincent is seen by his colleagues as direct and open about his likes and dislikes. He can be critical and abrasive in presenting his solutions to problems and in disagreements. He does little that is specifically designed to give face to others. Rather, he feels that his peers and direct reports will benefit more if his comments are direct.

Recent analysis of Vincent's management style by HR consultants revealed that his direct reports are uncomfortable with his interpersonal manner. He is seen as too aggressive and self-centered. The direct reports felt that Vincent makes decisions that bolster his own career and make him look good to the management team. They also felt that he is not a good team player. The analysis cited a bad marketing decision. Team members felt that Vincent was behind the decision, but he made his junior colleague take responsibility for it.

"Post '80s"—The Little Emperors

The "Post '80s" are a subset of the Young, Hungry Tigers and comprise Chinese born after 1980. The result of China's one-child policy, they are just beginning to graduate from college and enter the employment market.

Each is an "only" child—there are more than 100 million such young people in China today. Like only children everywhere, they tend to grow up being the center of attention and love in the family. As the Chinese say, in each family six older persons focus their love, attention, and spending on the one child (six because there are two parents, plus two sets of grandparents). Such children do not have the benefit of learning to share with siblings and so, as many Chinese observe, they tend to grow up being self-centered, egotistical, overconfident, and materialistic—all something of a departure from the values supposedly engendered by the state's socialist ideology. They do not like to suffer; they are not accustomed to "eating bitterness." But they do have abundant individualism and ambition.

However, this individualism does not necessarily mean independence from their families, especially given the six-adults-to-one-child ratio. Many HR recruiters share the observation that their Post '80s employees are constantly seeking their parents' counsel (e.g., when accepting a job title, salary, office location, etc.). Some recruiters have gone so far as to deal directly with the parents. And the parents' involvement does not end once their children are on board. One HR supervisor in a Taicang plant explained how he, on occasion, would have to meet with younger employees' parents when these workers encountered some issues or conflicts on the job. As it turned out, some of the young plant operators were raising their grievances about the company through their parents.

With no siblings and no need to share, the Post '80s Little Emperors tend to grow into young adults with few team skills, a flaw that is magnified by the education system. Children are allotted to universities, schools, or academic disciplines based solely on examination results. In other countries, schools use interviews and other assessment tools in addition to written exams to evaluate nonacademic interests and interpersonal skills.

How Do the Tigers Feel About Their Careers?

What goals do young, aspiring Chinese professionals have for their careers? Here are some results from DDI's *China Global Comparison—Leadership Forecast 2005–2006* survey:[4]

- **High percentage of strivers**—Almost all the leaders surveyed in China (98 percent) said they wanted to be promoted to higher levels of leadership—a percentage that has increased from survey to survey.

- **Very ambitious**—The leaders surveyed set audacious career goals and wanted to reach them in the shortest possible time. When asked about their motivation for climbing the ladder, 53 percent said the sooner the better, which is much higher than the global average of 35 percent. In terms of their material comforts, many felt that the gap between their current state and their desired state was huge. They wanted to climb the ladder as quickly and as early as possible because they believed that if they failed, it would be better to do so at a young age.

- **High energy**—They are willing to learn and work extra hard (longer hours, much travel)—even if it meant making personal sacrifices in their work-life balance. Their job decisions are often linked to training, learning opportunities, and potential for advancement.

- **Willing to take personal risk and make sacrifices**—Overall, 93 percent of those surveyed said they were willing to make personal sacrifices to get ahead, compared with 68 percent of the other global respondents. Almost half (45 percent) indicated that they give work a priority because they find it more fulfilling than their personal lives.

Strategizing for Success: A Profile of a Young, Ambitious Chinese Manager

At 29, Tam Wei is the chief financial officer of a world-renowned chain of do-it-yourself (DIY) stores in China. He is a business graduate, and this is his third job since graduation.

Tam has a clear, mechanistic view of his career path with well-defined strategies on how to achieve it—strategies that he openly shares with others. His basic advice is this: "Select a job in a new and booming industry. If you fail to do this, then select a new company in a mature industry. If this fails, then select a new job in an old company."

After graduation Tam selected a new job in a booming industry. He was hired as the personal assistant to the head of a local investment group and was mentored by one of the company's active owners.   Tam gained good professional experience as well as exposure to a network of other bankers. He was promoted to vice president at 25 because of his mentor's patronage, thus becoming one of the youngest investment banking vice presidents in China.   However, the company ran into serious trouble because of poor investment decisions, and its reputation and business plummeted.

This could have been a setback for Tam.   Instead, he viewed it as an opportunity to move to a more "structured" environment.   Recognizing the need to get more grounding as a business and functional executive, he carefully planned his next move and landed a job as a junior executive in the China operations of a top global accounting firm.   He moved up quickly, getting promoted from specialist consultant, to manager, to senior manager in only three years. Identified as a high-potential employee, he was selected for an overseas assignment in the United Kingdom, thus providing him with multinational, head office exposure. He used this position to land his current job with the DIY firm, which was a client of his while at the accounting firm.

According to Tam, "I pay much attention to, and put much effort into, building my portfolio of marketable skills. I ensure that each of my jobs builds on the next, so that I accumulate relevant skills to make myself more valuable and marketable with each move. There is no failure in the strictest sense. There are only temporary setbacks and difficulties, in my view."

How Promising Young Chinese Prioritize[5]

When asked to rank their education and initial career choices in order of importance, students at good universities in China today typically come up with a list that looks something like this (from most- to least-preferred choices):

1. Obtain a master's degree in the U.S., U.K., or Australia.
2. Work for a multinational company to be trained.
3. Work for a Chinese joint venture (JV) with a foreign company.
4. Obtain an advanced degree in China.
5. Work for a private Chinese company.
6. Work for a government, state-owned enterprise.

Another survey, this one by the British Council, confirms and extends DDI's *China Leadership Forecast* findings. This survey of 70,000 people, aged 16 to 39 living in 30 big cities, found that young Chinese are now very confident about their future and that they are pragmatic.[6] Many were interested in politics at their university—certainly, the 1989 pro-democracy movement and the lead-up to it were galvanizing—but with China's government permitting more freedoms, their idealism has turned to pragmatism. Now what they care most about is getting a good job and making money.

Researchers asked a number of questions about basic values. In many ways, the attitudes of young Chinese are not unlike those of young Americans in the post-World War II era. For instance:

- **Individualism**—About two-thirds of those surveyed indicated a preference to do things themselves, rather than rely on others. The same percentage also said they tend not to judge how others choose to live their lives.
- **Craving a better life**—Only 39 percent said they were happy with their current lives, and just 18 percent said they have enough money to enjoy life. Many (59 percent) said they need to take risks to be successful. For consumer products companies, this means that there is a strong desire for new trends and that brand loyalty is weak among the young.
- **Career ambition**—A large majority (80 percent) said they work very hard to advance in their career, and two-thirds agreed with the statement, "It is important that my family thinks I am successful."
- **Internationalism**—Two-thirds said they are interested in other cultures and international events, while 52 percent said they are attracted to the lifestyles of developed nations.

- **Value of knowledge**—Although 75 percent said it's important to be well informed, there is a direct link between the desire for information and the desire to advance one's career; information for its own sake is not appreciated. This attitude also explains why the education market—especially for business and professional improvement programs—is booming across China, as are business book sales.
- **Longing for enjoyment**—There is growing demand for leisure activities. Yet, the survey found that 51 percent are willing to sacrifice leisure for making more money. This suggests that the younger generation is still hardworking, although not quite as much as recent past generations.

The Rush to Be Middle Class

What most drives the career ambitions of young people in China? It's the desire to reach an income level that will give them a middle-class lifestyle as quickly as possible—certainly, at least as soon as their schoolmates do it. Not to do so could cause a loss of face in front of one's peers.

But what does it mean to be "middle class" in China? Salary of around RMB10,000 (USD1,375) a month is considered a middle-class income for a single person. A professional with a university degree in Beijing, Shanghai, or one of the coastal cities should expect to earn such a salary after three to five years in the workforce. About 20 percent of the Chinese workforce can be considered middle class. By 2025 that figure is expected to rise to 40 percent.

China's Women: Full Economic Participants

Those new to Asia might arrive with out-of-date notions about women's roles. Women do not automatically assume submissive or dependent roles. This was never the case in much of traditional Southeast Asia, and in China the Communist administration ensured that many restrictive practices regarding women were outlawed. Chairman Mao Zedong famously proclaimed that China's women "hold up half the sky." Under Mao they were given prominent roles in public administration and in state-owned enterprises, and schooling for all girls was made compulsory. This means that adult female literacy in China is relatively high—around 87 percent according to the last census (2000) compared with India, where it is 48 percent (from India's 2001 census).

Today, the demand for quality employees is so intense—particularly among foreign firms—that discrimination against women simply isn't economically feasible. And so women occupy many prominent positions in a whole range of sectors.

A 2006 report from Guanghua School of Management of Peking University found that women comprised almost 20 percent of leadership positions in China's business sector.[7] It also showed that 57 percent of women leaders believed that they can balance their family and work life. The gender composition of China's universities bears this out; at present, more than half (55.3 percent) of degree candidates in China's universities are female.[8]

Yang Mianmian, president of Haier Group, is a prominent example of a female business leader in China. In 2006 she ranked 20 in *Fortune* magazine's international list of the 50 most powerful women.[9] Much of Haier's success over the past two decades—transforming a Qingdao refrigerator factory to a $12.2 billion global home appliance giant—can be attributed to Yang's "one low, three high" strategy. (The "one" represents cost and the "three" represents value, growth, and quality.) Yang has pushed the company into international markets. For example, it now accounts for more than half of the small refrigerators sold in the U.S.

Dong Mingzhu, president of Gree Electric Appliances, is another powerful woman business leader cited by *Fortune*.[10] Under her leadership the company has grown from a small Zhuhai appliance maker to the world's leading manufacturer of household air conditioners. Its 2006 revenue rose 38 percent over the previous year to $1.7 billion. Dong, now in her fifties, started with the company as a sales representative.

Two more examples of women who have achieved positions of prominence are Wang Jiafen, chairman of Bright Dairy Products Group, and Tang Meijuan, CEO of TOM, China's leading wireless Internet company.

Rapid economic growth also has been important for mobilizing women into the paid workforce at lower levels. Currently, half of all internal female migrant workers in China head to the manufacturing-for-export regions of Guangdong Province and the Pearl River Delta. Employers prefer young women for assembly line work because they are nimble and pay attention to detail.

Anecdotally, many managers believe women are less likely to behave poorly when acting in an official capacity than are men. Also, they are better at complying with corporate governance measures. Whereas men might be seen as visionary and "big picture" thinkers, women are seen as more careful in complying with regulations and auditing requirements. As a result, it is no surprise that women are more prominent than men in China (and around Asia) in accounting, auditing, and human resources departments.

A Western expatriate in China who runs a public relations agency remarked that one of the good things about his business is that most of his client contacts are women. To him, that means fewer opportunities to end up in compromising situations; there is less need to be a part of China's "macho" business culture, which requires heavy drinking sessions and karaoke singing, usually in the company of *xiaojies,* or bar hostesses. Instead, business socializing with his female clients occurs over lunch and coffee, allowing negotiations to be carried out in a more measured, less pressured environment, away from alcohol. His negotiations are more straightforward too, with fewer requests for "commissions" and other inappropriate financial payments. And there are fewer entertainment expense claims—dubious or otherwise.

All of this is not to say that there is no discrimination against women in China. Rules and regulations concerning discrimination are less likely to be observed in more remote and rural areas; but certainly, along China's coastal strip and in the cities, women play very active social and commercial roles.

One consequence of women's growing workforce participation is that China's divorce rate is rising.[11] It now stands at about 15 percent, but it is higher and rising faster in urban areas. Economic opportunities for women mean that they need not be financially dependent on men and are increasingly more able to exit an unhappy marriage.

The Great Leap Forward . . . from State to Private Enterprise

Eva is making a move from a state-owned enterprise to a private company. Not only does this involve a change of employer, but Eva also must move to a different city. She has 10 years' experience in a well-run, profitable state enterprise, but decided to make the move because the new job will give her an opportunity to use the latest technology in her professional discipline as well as more learning opportunities and exposure to new ideas and methods. She knows it is a big jump, but she is determined to seize the opportunity. Very quickly, she sees a big difference between the work practices and culture of the state-owned enterprise and the private company.

Factors	State Enterprise	Private Company
Focus	Internally focused.	Customer focused.
Work pace	Work at your own pace; that is, relatively slower.	Work at client's pace— usually fast.
Output	Activity driven; mostly qualitative performance indicators.	Output driven; quantitative performance indicators.
Performance reward	Rewards based on "seniority" of service.	Rewards based on individual performance, and there is differentiation of rewards.
Frequency of change	Few changes; work flow and assignments change infrequently.	Frequent changes; the individual is required to apply learning in many new situations.
Complexity of work	Singular and functional assignments; not much integration with other areas is needed.	Need a great deal of integration and collaboration among teams.
Pressure of work	Low, controlled by the individual.	Extremely high, not controlled by the individual.

With all these new challenges for her and her family, Eva still firmly believes that her decision to relocate for the sake of the new job is the right one, and she will make it successful. With all the benefits Eva hopes success will bring, failure is not an option.

Your Toughest Assignment

As an expatriate, successfully managing people from outside your own culture is one of the toughest assignments you will ever have in your career. You must spend a significant amount of time thinking not just about what you say to people, but also how you will say it. Face is important in China, and people are quick to take offense, but not necessarily visibly so. To a large extent, the people you manage will determine your success or failure in China, so understanding them and their backgrounds will be an essential component of your time in China. You hold the key to their success as employees, just as they hold the key to your success. HR issues will never matter to you more than in China.

CHAPTER 3

Attracting Qualified Applicants

E ach year millions of students graduate from China's more than 1,000 tertiary institutions. While college graduates are not in short supply, *quality* graduates are another matter—competition for them is very fierce in China. It is a candidate's market. So how do you get high-caliber candidates to select you and your company as their employer of choice? What makes a company attractive to prospective candidates? What turns them off? And how do you differentiate between good and average applicants? This chapter addresses these questions.

Branding Your Company to Attract Applicants

The Chinese are very brand conscious—not simply with respect to their selection of expensive items, such as designer-label clothing, but also relative to minor consumer decisions, such as choosing dishwashing detergent. And so it is with prospective employees: Companies with well-known brands, such as Intel, IBM, Microsoft, Deloitte Touche Tohmatsu, and Procter & Gamble, attract lots of job applications. It is not unheard of for these super brands to attract up to 50,000 applicants each during their campus recruitment season.

More than anything, a brand represents the company's reputation. Chinese employees want to feel proud when they show their business card to their relatives and peers; they want a reputable company's name to impress. Working in such an organization gives face not only to the person concerned, but also to his or her entire family. It's common for young graduates to seek their parents' views about the employment offers they receive. Parents want to be proud to tell their neighbors, friends, or competing members of the extended family about their son's or daughter's job.

The name along with the reputation of the hiring company also becomes an asset for the new employee in his or her process of extending personal connections, known as *guanxi,* a term that also connotes the desire to achieve harmony between individuals and organizations. Attachment to a strong brand also suggests marketable skills. "If you work for Microsoft, you can get into any company" is a commonly held attitude. People will want to know employees with such connections, which, in turn, will expand their network and the opportunities that flow from having a good network.

Also, to most Chinese a strong brand represents world-class technology—and that represents learning opportunities. Chinese employees are eager to learn the best and newest technology from the outside world. Candidates seek out companies where they will be able to learn or strengthen valuable skills that will boost their ability to get better jobs in the future. Therefore, jobs requiring Internet-based software programming, R&D, and investment analysis are in demand. New graduates understand that China is becoming a global player in the world economy and that there will be huge demand for those who are well versed not only in Chinese culture but also in modern (Western) technology.

In short, foreign companies with well-known names do not have a problem attracting quality applicants. A 2006 survey by the Corporate Leadership Council (CLC) of 11,124 students from 60 top Chinese universities found that the five most sought-after employers by engineering/IT graduates are IBM, China Mobile, Microsoft, Google, and Procter & Gamble. Business graduates' most preferred employers are Procter & Gamble, McKinsey, Citigroup, HSBC, and China Mobile.[1]

And the Winner Is . . .

Several corporations enjoy excellent reputations among graduates from good schools in China. These companies do not need to invest heavily in recruiting because the top-flight graduates find them. Their mentoring and training programs are big attractions.

Procter & Gamble (P&G) epitomizes this kind of employer. It offers an excellent graduate training program in China and has a strong global brand name. P&G consistently ranks as one of the most desirable employers. Respondents in a 2007 CLC survey ranked it third when asked to nominate their ideal employer. Business-related majors ranked it number one. And it was ranked number two by 90,000 respondents in 600 universities in a survey that same year by ChinaHR.com.[2]

Some organizations and sectors that are not seen as glamorous or desirable employers by many high-quality graduates in the West are coveted by young, ambitious Chinese graduates. Starbucks, Pizza Hut, and McDonald's are examples. To young Chinese, these are world-class employers in terms of their customer service standards and use of technology. More than anything, these companies represent learning and training opportunities, and their management techniques are first-class. Many in China are eager to learn from them and apply such skills—not just in Chinese fast-food chains, but also in other, similarly structured organizations.

Companies that do not have well-known brands still can attract quality candidates if they offer marketable skills, are staffed via an impressive selection system, and provide good training in management and technology.

Training is a highly attractive lure for many promising young graduates. Often, it is their main consideration. Says one consultant, "I was running a high-potential leadership development forum for a multinational company with a large presence in China, and I was providing a coaching session to one of the participants, who I'm sure will eventually become a general manager. When I found out that he had been recruited from another multinational company within the past six months, I asked him why—what had caused him to switch jobs? It wasn't the pay, his leader in the old position, or the company strategy; instead, it was his new company's reputation as an organization that invests in its people through innovative development offerings." This is not an unusual occurrence in China.

What Job Sectors Are Preferred?

Engineering graduates most prefer R&D jobs and sales engineering positions; manufacturing is a less-enticing choice. Positions in R&D often attract hundreds of applicants with master's degrees, while few master's graduates will apply for other engineering positions. Business graduates look for professional firms, such as international consulting companies and accounting firms that have well-defined professional progression. Marketing jobs that have international exposure are next in order of preference.

Most Chinese parents, like parents the world over, perceive jobs that require their sons and daughters to use their brains to be much more prestigious than jobs that require specialist operating skills. An electronic technician might earn more than an office worker, but in China, more face is earned from being an office worker.

China Graduates' Most-Preferred Job Sectors[3] (by All Graduates)

When asked, "In which industries would you ideally like to work?" university graduates, selecting a maximum of three industries, chose the following:

1. Management Consulting (18.3 percent)
2. Investment Banking (16.1 percent)
3. Government/Public Service (15.4 percent)
4. Academic Research (14.8 percent)
5. Education/Training (14.2 percent)

What Employer Nationalities Are Preferred?

Another way in which prospective Chinese employees rank their employer preferences relates to where the employer is based. U.S. and European companies are ranked highest. Young Chinese tend not to differentiate among U.S., British, French, or German companies—what is important is that they are Western. Candidates learn through both word of mouth and published salary surveys that U.S. and European companies pay better, provide better working environments, and offer better medical and other benefits, particularly when compared with companies that are headquartered in Asia. For more junior levels, all companies pay the same benefits as required by local labor laws, but Western companies typically provide better medical benefits than are required by law.

What Types of Managers Are Preferred?

Young Chinese university graduates generally prefer jobs in which their direct supervisor is a Western expatriate. Expatriates are perceived as having superior professional knowledge and experience. Those from English-speaking countries are preferred because working with them affords Chinese employees greater opportunities to improve their English skills.

Rarely do Western managers have difficulty attracting local applicants for secretarial positions. Western bosses are preferred to local ones because local secretarial staff feel that they will be of more use (and perhaps have more power) if their bosses are not proficient in Chinese and therefore will be more dependent on them.

What Don't Young Graduates Like?

Multinational organizations are the most desirable employers for ambitious, young Chinese graduates, but there are exceptions. Shift work is abhorred, particularly if it involves night work. This is due in part to a traditional belief that working nights harms your health. Also, it works against their strong family values. Finally, shift work is seen as "low class" and thus harmful to one's face.

Relocating away from parents is difficult. Young graduates nearly always prefer to live with their parents, even if they have to commute some distance to work each day, rather than live near their work location. Moving risks dishonoring their parents and possibly not being around while they age. The sense of duty with which Chinese regard their parents cannot be underestimated.

Companies with poor reputations are avoided. Word of mouth, the Internet, and inflammatory and sensationalist press reports all can quickly damage a company's reputation in China today. Perceptions of social corporate responsibility and employee welfare remain important in China. Appearing to be excessively profit driven will harm a company's image as an employer; after all, China ostensibly remains a socialist country. Similarly, companies that have downsized in the past or have had legal disputes with local employees are seen as lacking sufficient long-term commitment to China; they, too, will find it more difficult to attract the best candidates.

What Do Young Graduates Like?

As mentioned earlier, training opportunities are very important for attracting potential employees. The degree to which a particular job is viewed as a stepping stone to the next also is significant. But this is not to say that starting salary and related benefits are not also important. In the 2006 CLC survey, 58 percent of the graduates rated compensation as the number one priority in selecting a job.[4]

Increasingly, Chinese graduates prefer to receive more of their compensation as a performance-related bonus (59 percent, according to the CLC). This suggests greater confidence in their self-worth as well as their growing individualism and competitiveness. By way of comparison, similar surveys in Southeast Asia show that local employees rarely want their pay to be linked to their individual performance. And several Western-owned Chinese companies report a preference by their non-management workers for group (team) incentives over individual incentives. There seem to be large regional differences in how team incentives are viewed.

Half (52 percent) of respondents in the CLC survey rated medical and health care benefits as second in importance after salary. The desire for health care protection reflects the rising cost of health care in China as it moves from the relatively poor state-provided health care services to a user-pays system. Additional private coverage is very necessary in China, even for young people.

The same CLC report showed that candidates consider career prospects as the third most important criteria—after compensation and benefits—in selecting a job. Graduates are attracted to employers that have well-defined career paths. They want an indication of how soon they can reach a management position. They also want exposure to overseas training or assignments and assurance that the company has a long-term commitment to China.

Learning Paths Can Be Substituted for Career Paths

Many Western organizations operating in China are relatively flat, making it difficult to show an exciting career path in the time frame that many university graduates would like. Some organizations give the illusion of a career path by creating a hierarchy of job titles that are unrelated to actual responsibility changes.

A better system would be to have a visible (either paper or online) "learning path" that shows specific knowledge and skills that an employee can acquire at different intervals. Learning paths graphically portray the learning opportunities awaiting a graduate and give the person a chance to gauge upward progress. Organizations using a learning path often illustrate the concept with a stair-step graphic with catchy names for each step.

Some multinationals attract quality graduates with promises of six-month training stints at the head office in the U.S. or Europe. In the CLC survey 47 percent of respondents mentioned international training and travel opportunities as being important to them when choosing a job. Often, graduates will openly admit that an offer of six months of overseas training is the only or main reason for accepting a position. It is a "carrot" that mainland companies cannot offer and that Taiwanese companies can, but only without guarantee because business visas to Taiwan are still subject to restrictions and uncertainty.

Why do young Chinese hold overseas training and exposure in such high regard? Not so much for the sake of travel outside China, but because they feel that outside exposure will give them an edge on their competitors. When Chinese employees go overseas for training, it is not unusual for them to work 14-hour days, 7 days a week, to maximize what they can learn during their stay.

But a word of caution: It is common for individuals to leave an employer upon their return from a foreign assignment. To help prevent this, the individual's real motivation should be thoroughly investigated as part of the selection system (see Chapter 4).

Another important factor in job acceptance is the *hukou,* or residential permit for big cities, without which the future education of employees' children might be affected. Companies that can help arrange such permits create a significant lure in attracting good staff away from other cities. For instance, a northeastern student will see a residential permit for Shanghai as a highly coveted benefit for the future.

The Role of the *Hukou* in Attracting Staff

Born and raised in Heilongjiang Province, Xin Yan is intelligent, and while she attended Harbin Institute of Technology for an electrical engineering degree, she participated in a number of extracurricular activities. Similar to Georgia Institute of Technology or Carnegie Mellon University in the United States, Harbin Institute of Technology is widely recognized as one of the top universities in China.

Upon graduation, Xin Yan becomes a candidate for selection by a prominent high-tech manufacturing company. She does well in the assessments for cognitive skills (analytical thinking) and assessments using job simulations that evaluate interpersonal and managerial skills. She also impresses her interviewer with her record of extracurricular activities, which further demonstrate these qualities.

Xin Yan scores in the top 10 percentile of candidates in the applicant pool and is offered a position with a good starting salary and six months of classroom and on-the-job training. But what entices her most is the promise that the company will arrange an application for a *hukou* (residential permit) for Shanghai. This *hukou* will entitle her child (when she has one) to study in Shanghai schools as a local citizen. (School fees for non-local citizens are extravagantly high.) In Xin Yan's mind, the opportunity for her child to study in a big city such as Shanghai will improve the outlook of her family's next generation. Although this benefit will only accrue in later years, she believes it would be wise to get the *hukou* now.

Fast-growing cities like Shanghai need well-trained professionals like Xin Yan, so they prioritize internal migrants with certain skills. Companies tend to sponsor the applications of prospective employees' *hukou,* but some are better than others at obtaining the permits.

Finally, graduates see a company's long-term commitment to change and innovation as highly desirable. Most want to be associated with a company that is agile and cutting edge, that is capable of staying abreast of new developments, and that promises to remain competitive. Change means opportunity—something that China's young, promising graduates have come to embrace.

University Campaigns and Visits

Many organizations find it fruitful to tap into the supply of quality graduates at their source—by visiting the better universities themselves. Such visits allow companies to make career presentations to target groups of students. To initiate these visits, companies can contact a university's employment or career offices, which must be consulted well in advance of the visit.

Some employment agencies in China specialize in finding entry-level graduates. They also can be helpful in arranging campus visits, as they can assist with pre-visit promotion activities and liaison work with the university career office. In some provinces the government has affiliate organizations that support campus career activities. These tend to have better relationships with the universities than do most private agents. In 2006 a job fair in Zhengzhou attracted so many people to the conference center that the escalator and doors bent under the stampede of students.

Although September, October, and November are the highest-volume recruiting months, recruiting and relationship building (e.g., providing speakers and guest lecturers) are year-round efforts. In fact, more companies are starting earlier each year in order to beat the competition to acquire the best talent.

What can companies do to get themselves noticed so that they can attract top candidates? Be creative! Recently, one company that was looking to hire 24 management trainees from one of the best MBA programs in China billed its half-day selection process as a "unique experience that will provide meaningful career and life insights for participants." The HR group partnered with the marketing team to create enough "buzz" around the event that it was able to attract more than 200 highly qualified, fresh graduates for the half-day assessment center-based selection process.

During the Organization Presentation Sessions

When representing the organization on campus, ideally an expatriate and a local Chinese manager should make the presentation together. The expatriate manager should focus on describing the company's growth opportunities, its strategic plan in China, and the company's vision and values. The local Chinese manager should explain the job positions, types of formal training, career opportunities, and the related selection process.

Candidates will expect to hear about career and development opportunities, the company's financial and technological successes, and its future plans. An organization's future plans are most important in candidates' decision-making processes. Young Chinese graduates are aware of multinational companies failing in China and furloughing their employees. They want to be reassured that they will be joining a winning organization with a bright future.

Many young Chinese also have nationalistic sympathies. They are unlikely to be impressed by companies that come to China only for the "market," for "profits," or for "low labor costs." They are committed to China, and they would like to feel that their employer is too. Therefore, it would be beneficial for the foreign company to explain how it is contributing to the economic and social development of China, perhaps by bringing in new technology or by opening an R&D center. This information is best delivered in person by an expatriate manager—not a local Chinese. Again, the nationality of the firm needs to be emphasized in a constructive way. Energetic presentations will be well received.

Personal stories are best used to demonstrate career prospects within the company. Presenters should talk about their own progression through the organization; this tends to personalize the content and make the presenter more accessible to prospective employees who need to be engaged emotionally. Another good idea would be to include in the presentation local Chinese graduates who have joined the company and made significant progress in two or three years, showcasing their own professional success. Again, this personalizes the presentation and allows prospective candidates to identify with the message, rather than see it as a sales pitch.

Recruiting Via the Internet

Increasingly, Chinese students and other job seekers are going to the Internet to get information about job opportunities and to learn about specific companies that are offering jobs. Smart companies offer attractive web sites in the Chinese language. More and more companies (e.g., Procter & Gamble) use the Web not only to inform, but also to screen candidates. Individuals interested in jobs take a series of online tests to help them consider their capabilities and motivations for the jobs that are open. Web sites that allow an individual to compare his or her own skills with particular job requirements are highly attractive to Chinese applicants. For example, an organization might ask a series of questions that are focused on an individual's motivations, and then present the profile back to the person along with a profile that has been developed from surveys of the company's most successful people in that position. That way, the applicant can determine if he or she would be a good motivational fit for the position. The applicant may continue in the selection process even if he or she is not a good fit for the job. However, most who fail to match the particular profile wanted by an organization tend to drop out.

Applicants can get to an organization's web site either directly or indirectly. If the organization is well known, the applicant may just choose to investigate it. More commonly, applicants can go to a web-based recruiting system, such as 51job.com, ChinaHR.com, Monster.com, or those operated by the popular Chinese search engine Baidu.com, to find organizations with job openings requiring skills that match their own.

Mounting an All-Out Recruitment Campaign

For an Established Company in China

A multistep approach is required to attract and screen candidates for those companies that have a well-established presence in China. (See Chapter 4.) This can be done by HR staff, or outside help can be obtained. Pre-campus coordination and promotion activities might be outsourced to a reliable specialist agent. The organization can appoint an agent to perform all the required logistical arrangements and initial web screenings using predetermined tests and simulations. The company's hiring managers then can focus on screened candidates and spend more time in deep discussions with them about career aspirations and employment opportunities.

Established organizations should not underestimate the power of word of mouth in attracting top-flight candidates. As has been mentioned, during campus visits companies can use current employees as "ambassadors" to sell themselves to target groups of graduates. Some companies set up employee-referral programs to attract new staff. The hiring rate of the candidates referred by current employees tends to be much higher because existing employees know the company culture and informally help to prescreen those who are most likely to fit into it. The retention rate of internal referrals also is higher.

For a Company New to China

A company that is new to China or relatively unknown should do two things when it comes to recruitment:

- Determine which cities to focus on.
- Decide which few universities to target.

Graduates from top universities in developed cities, like Beijing and Shanghai, have higher expectations for their career advancement and starting salaries. It might be prudent to consider students from inner cities who also might be of high caliber but have more modest career and salary expectations.

A good approach for an organization would be to establish strong relationships with three to four universities. China has more than a thousand universities; focusing on too many will spread the recruitment effort too thinly. Relationships with universities in China are like any relationships—they need time and effort to become mutually beneficial. Recruitment efforts also need to focus on individuals within an institution and not just on the institution itself. But which universities should be targeted? Many sources should be consulted to get a feel for the quality of the specific disciplines of graduates, and the list should be reviewed annually based on the previous year's success. Companies would be wise to move from universities that have not proven fruitful to others that might be.

New companies should make every attempt to create a positive image at campus interviews. Interviewing as many candidates as possible during a day can be tempting. Some organizations make the mistake of having hiring managers spend less than 10 or 15 minutes with each candidate. This creates the impression that interviewers—and hence the company—are not "serious" about knowing the candidates and giving face to them. It would be wise to be sensitive to the fact that candidates might have waited several hours to be seen. An interview of only 10 minutes will create disappointment on their side. Therefore, having appropriate tools, such as candidate testing, to screen out unsuitable interviewees at an early stage is a must. Such a practice would allow interviewers to spend more time with high-potential applicants.

Screening candidates to a manageable number helps to create a positive image for the company, provided the screening is done creatively and the test items or simulations are obviously job related.

Providing candidates with a positive interview experience helps companies new to China to develop a good reputation. Students often write about and share their interview experiences (both pleasant and otherwise) via the Internet.

Advertising can be used for more junior positions. Targeted newspaper recruitment ads are an option. Ads also can be placed in recruitment newspapers that are given away by the thousands, often in subway stations on Saturday mornings. One company has found success in filling more junior positions by placing ads on notice boards in 7-Eleven stores. Middle-class Chinese patronize such convenience stores, so this tactic reaches its intended demographic target. Table 3.1 reflects recruitment campaign practices from various multinational companies (MNCs).

TABLE 3.1: How to Attract Job Applicants

Strategy	"How to" Tactics
Employee Branding	• If working for an MNC, look to employee-branding best practices from corporate and around the world. Leverage what exists and tailor it to local needs. • Work with your internal marketing department to create a local employee brand. This usually is the greatest untapped weapon in the war for talent. • For campus visits, contract local PR firms that specialize in customizing a company brand. A word of caution—many offer a generic service that does not differentiate your company from the competition. • Hire staffing specialists from companies who are known for their employee brand. Welcome their new influences and different perspectives.
Sell the Company and Process	• Provide incentives for employee referrals. • Establish strong relationships with headhunters who are well connected in your industry. • Hold hiring managers accountable for selling the company and its culture during the interview. Allocate time in the interview process to provide the employment value proposition; at the very least, this will be the message candidates take back to friends and colleagues. • Demonstrate an efficient selection process, highlighting transparency and equity. • Articulate the company's development culture through clear career/learning paths.

TABLE 3.1 (cont'd): How to Attract Job Applicants

Strategy	"How to" Tactics
Understand What Works	• Create lead and lag measures to analyze what works and does not work for your company. Use the data to refine your sourcing strategy. Too many companies blindly set their sourcing strategies.
	• Understand what your competition is doing to attract talent. Leverage industry best practices, but strive to differentiate your company.
	• Do not rely solely on old beliefs as truths; for example, understand that school name/reputation does not always equate to the best employee.

This chapter has examined a range of strategies to get candidates to choose your organization. In the daily recruitment war that employers face in today's China, making promising candidates aware of your company and then having them choose it as a potential employer is half the battle. The other half is selecting the best candidates once they have chosen your organization. That is the subject of the next chapter.

CHAPTER 4

Selecting Your Team

A lot of expatriate managers coming to China underestimate the amount of time, commitment, and effort that will be required to select and hire their China team. And yet, this is the most important task that any expatriate manager will face, given how quickly China is developing and the current state of the labor market for quality, local professionals and people with leadership potential. This point has been made before in these pages, but is well worth making again.

As an expatriate manager, selecting your team in China is one leadership task that should not be delegated, no matter how time consuming it is. Some senior managers spend 40 percent of their first two years in China selecting their teams. No matter how long it takes, one thing is sure: It will take longer than you hope it will.

Getting the right team largely determines your success and happiness in China. Get it wrong, and much of your time will be spent on endless HR problems—day-to-day minutiae that will never let you focus on the big picture. Employee turnover will rise, and that will bring new problems such as the loss of proprietary information and even legal problems from disgruntled staff. The more sensationalistic of China's media love to run stories about some foreign company mistreating its staff—regardless of the facts—so you might end up with a public relations catastrophe too.

DDI's 2005 survey, *Leadership in China: Keeping Pace with a Growing Economy,* found that about 3 of 10 new employees were not considered good hiring decisions by the managers surveyed.[1] Such a ratio is unacceptable, particularly for organizations that are trying to expand rapidly.

Will this or that person be a successful leader of a Chinese team? It is a common quandary facing expatriate managers when trying to hire a local Chinese employee or manager. Determining a candidate's language proficiencies, technical knowledge, and previous job challenges can be relatively straightforward compared with assessing his or her motivation and interpersonal and leadership skills. Many expatriate managers feel helpless because they cannot use the hiring criteria from their past experiences (say in Germany or Australia) as a basis for a local hiring decision. These issues are covered in this chapter.

Hiring Traps in China

So what are the common mistakes made when hiring in China?

Yielding to the Pressure to Fill Positions

When there is pressure to fill positions, hiring managers are tempted to accept the best of a bad lot rather than continue searching for truly qualified applicants.

Having Too Few Qualified Candidates

The judgment of hiring managers can be influenced by the relative quality of applicants. Interviewers tend to rate an average applicant more favorably in a tight labor market where there are few qualified candidates.

Making Language Capability the Main Selection Criteria

The ability to speak the company's official language (usually English) is a legitimate hiring criterion. Thus, many expatriate managers use lack of proficiency in English-language skills to screen out applicants. But how good must language skills be when people start? Does the organization have the ability to check on aptitude for learning English (or another language)? And will the organization support language skill-development efforts? These questions are important because requiring a high level of English proficiency significantly limits the pool of candidates for most jobs in China.

Hiring managers in China have to make a decision about required language skills for every job they fill. Is speaking English a "must have" or a "nice to have"? Are there successful people in the job who do not have English-language skills? How will the lack of those skills affect individuals' chances for promotion or transfer? Is it more important to have salespeople who speak English or salespeople who are effective on the job?

Equating Language Capability with Managerial Skills

Speaking English proficiently does not mean a person will be a good manager, yet many expatriates make this mistake. They find someone with whom they can have good conversations, and they attribute to them all sorts of other positive attributes, such as motivation, initiative, and, most important, people skills. Many Chinese managers have to speak English because they are the linchpin between the non-English-speaking Chinese and the rest of the organization. But many expatriate managers have found that having a direct report who is really good with people is more important than one who is fluent in the organization's home language.

Relying Too Heavily on Training to Fill Skill Gaps

In a tight labor market, it's very easy for managers to rationalize their hiring of unqualified people, thinking, "We will train this person later on." Managers must take a realistic look at what they can develop in individuals and what they can't. For example, certain personality attributes are very difficult to change.

There's no question that many leadership skills can be developed. The issue is, will the new hire be given the necessary time, instruction, and coaching to develop them? Often the answer is no. Expatriate managers must resist the temptation to fool themselves about their organization's ability to develop people and, thus, lower their hiring standards.

On the other hand, if people have been selected properly relative to their ability and motivation to learn, then there is a good chance an investment in the development of those individuals would be beneficial. In these cases people with lower technical or leadership skills can be brought into an organization and put on a development path.

Language and technical skills seem to be more developable than many interpersonal skills. Often, because the development of those skills can be more easily outsourced, people can be sent to language or technical schools. Many individuals who are hired with limited English skills develop perfectly adequate language skills over time. The key words are "over time." Often, it takes several years for people to build the necessary skills. But they are in a perfect situation—they're getting formal instruction and ample opportunity to practice. The ability to learn language skills can be accurately predicted through language aptitude tests and interviews that assess "motivation to learn." So, it is *personal attributes* (e.g., personal development orientation and learning ability) that many employers might want to test for, rather than language proficiency alone.

Setting Hiring Qualifications Too High

Another common hiring mistake made by expatriate managers is setting hiring qualifications too high. This can happen because China has no shortage of college and university graduates. All too often, graduates or college students are hired to do jobs that don't require that level of education. Employing graduates in basic administrative or simple customer service roles will lead them to feel bored and underutilized, which, in turn, will encourage them to seek employment elsewhere. Or it might lead them to secretly operate their own businesses from your premises in their spare time.

Placing Too Much Stock in an MBA

Many applicants in China now have an MBA or are in the process of completing one. While an MBA is important, it provides no guarantee that people have the skills they need to succeed in a given position. Around Asia there is a tendency to see an MBA as a piece of paper to be acquired, rather than as an indication that new workplace skills have been learned. Too often, those who obtain a local or foreign MBA know *what* to do in business or interpersonal situations but not *how* to do it, because they lack behavioral skills. Coaching is an example; few MBA programs teach would-be managers how to effectively coach people.

Nonetheless, an MBA can be quite meaningful. It can be an indicator of motivation, learning ability, and understanding of business terms and concepts. And while it can be a good indicator of quality, an MBA is not a perfect barometer. This caveat is particularly important to expatriate managers who don't recognize the vast differences in the quality of MBA programs in China, as described in Chapter 2.

Relying Too Heavily on University and College Results

Organizations everywhere select young talent based on their university results. But in China there are thousands of universities and colleges, ranging from those that are almost comparable to better Western universities to those that are downright appalling. More than 5 million Chinese graduate from universities each year—a number that is rising exponentially. But the vast majority are nowhere near comparable academically to the average Western graduate. And it is difficult to discern the good from the bad. For example, as mentioned earlier some famous universities have franchised their good names to lesser institutions in order to have access to more fee-paying students. Also, as will be discussed later, the falsification of qualifications and certificates is rampant.

Hiring Family or Customer Referrals

Jobs often are allocated in China on the basis of *guanxi*—personal contacts and networks. Many firms in China hire people because they are related to some government official or an important customer. In the course of business, curricula vitae (CVs) often are received with a note asking if something can be done to hire a cousin, niece, nephew, etc. Expatriate managers often acquiesce and ask their HR departments to see if some unimportant position can be found for the "connected" person. The temptation for an easy fix needs to be carefully considered. Helping an official or a customer might yield short-term benefits, but cause longer-term damage. Following such a practice can be akin to maintaining a dam: Operations can become silted up with staff employed for reasons other than merit; ultimately, the quality staff will overflow the dam wall in search of a more agile, merit-based working environment.

A Qualified Referral?

Patricia is in the third week of her expatriate assignment in China. At the end of the weekly staff meeting, her marketing manager, Chui Bao, wants to discuss a job candidate recommended by a customer.

Having noticed some performance problems within the marketing team and recognizing that it could benefit from the influx of quality talent, Patricia is happy to listen.

After reviewing the candidate's background and experience, Chui mentions that the candidate comes highly recommended by Mark, one of the company's key customers. "In summary," Chui says, "The candidate is great, fantastic."

"In what ways?" Patricia asks. Chui cannot be specific, and his face turns crimson. Patricia knows that hiring the right person is a very important decision for the organization, so she doesn't give in. She insists on behavioral evidence of the candidate's skills.

Hiring for Business or Political Relationships

Another hiring mistake is to select staff mainly because they will bring *guanxi*—that their extensive network of connections will be immediately useful to the company. *Guanxi* is important, but it also carries considerable risk. Someone might have potentially useful *guanxi*, but does he or she also have personal integrity and the time management, planning, and organizational skills required? Furthermore, in China good *guanxi* can go bad very quickly. The relationships of a niece of a vice mayor might not be so valuable should the vice mayor be arrested for corruption and face a long jail term or even execution.

A Case of Good *Guanxi,* but Poor Fit

Edmund was recruited to the public relations department of an international media company. He was a university graduate with three years' experience working at a reputable international hotel in Shanghai. After his experience at the hotel, Edmund wanted to work in a different industry.

Edmund's new manager selected him because of his relationships with government and government-related organizations. The hiring manager felt that Edmund's connections and strong interpersonal skills would be useful to the company.

During the first three months on the job, Edmund's performance was outstanding. He demonstrated initiative and a high energy level in meetings.

But by the fifth month, Edmond started to behave differently. He became more selective about his assignments, not wanting to do more routine tasks and working only on the assignments that he liked. He did not enjoy working with other team members; instead, he wanted to spend almost all of his time cultivating external relationships.

By the eighth month, Edmund's manager was concerned about his behavior. He was charming with those outside the company whom he wanted to cultivate, but internally he was brusque with colleagues—particularly those in whom he was not interested. His manager also heard from an external source that Edmund might have some problems with "integrity." There was talk that Edmund was using the company's name to develop his own outside business interests. For the company that hired him, Edmund's *guanxi* came at a cost.

Falling for Self-Promoters

Chinese candidates are relatively adept at selling themselves in interviews; ambitious, young graduates tend to know how to position their capabilities or, in some cases, the capabilities they feel they should have. They are skilled at "impression management." Hiring organizations have three remedies for this:

- Conducting behavior-based interviews that focus on evidence of past performance and accomplishments.
- Supplementing interviews with validated tests and simulations to obtain objective insights.
- Spending time on careful reference checks.

These remedies will be described in more detail later in this chapter.

Taking Assessment Shortcuts

Developing and maintaining a structured, consistent selection system takes commitment and effort. Time pressures in China often push managers to circumvent their organization's selection system at the expense of sound hiring and promotion decisions. For example, they try to interview people in 15 minutes, or before making a hiring decision, they spend only one or two minutes exchanging insights with the interviewers who have met with the candidate.

Allowing Untrained Interviewers to Make Decisions

Some managers allow their people to assume responsibility for hiring and promoting others when they have not acquired for themselves the necessary skills for properly assessing people. Untrained interviewers often will draw conclusions about others based on subjective biases or on how candidates sell themselves in an interview.

So how do you avoid hiring traps in China? Read on.

How to Hire in China

Universal hiring principles hold true in China as much as anywhere. The seven fundamental rules are:

1. Establish a Success Profile^{SM} for the position or level.
2. Develop a structured, efficient selection process to obtain data on the components of the Success Profile for the target position or level.
3. Hire for job fit motivation and cultural fit motivation in addition to job skills.
4. Train managers to be effective interviewers.
5. Use tests, targeted simulations, assessment centers, and reference checks to supplement interview data.
6. Train managers to make accurate hiring decisions using all available information.
7. Set up a system to monitor adherence to the selection process and the organization's selection standards.

1. Establish a Success Profile℠ for the Position or Level

The first step in any selection system is to define the system's targets—what it takes to succeed. Development Dimensions International (DDI) calls this a *Success Profile*. For a particular assignment or program (e.g., a high-potential program), a Success Profile has four components:

- Competencies (i.e., behavior)
- Job challenges (i.e., specific experiences)
- Knowledge (e.g., an MBA)
- Personal attributes (e.g., motivation)

Figure 4.1 depicts the components of a Success Profile. Each component is described on the next few pages.

Figure 4.1: Components of a Success Profile℠

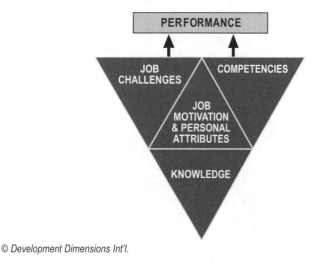

© Development Dimensions Int'l.

A well-conceived Success Profile focuses selection efforts on the most important areas and prevents managers from being swayed by a single criterion (e.g., strong English ability or good connections). Just as a desirable candidate will not be one dimensional, neither should the selection system.

Behaviorally Defined Competencies

Competencies (also called dimensions) define clusters of behavior that are related to job success or failure. Examples of interpersonal competencies include:

- Building Strategic Relationships
- Building Trust
- Communicating with Impact
- Customer Orientation
- Persuasiveness/Sales Ability

Some leadership competencies include:

- Change Leadership
- Coaching/Teaching
- Delegation
- Developing Organizational Talent
- Empowerment

Job Challenges

The term *job challenges*—rather than job experience—best describes what interviewers should be looking for. Too often, interviewers are fooled by an applicant's job experience. Someone who has been a salesperson for many years is not necessarily a good salesperson and might have been doing a different kind of selling (e.g., transactional selling when the target position requires consultative selling).

Job challenges encompass the kinds of situations that a person needs to have dealt with in order to succeed in the target job. Examples include carrying out an assignment from beginning to end, implementing a companywide change, negotiating agreements with other organizations, and operating in high-pressure, high-visibility situations.

Job challenges are not very important in hiring university graduates directly out of school, because most of them have not had an opportunity to encounter the kinds of challenges they will face on the job. However, job challenges are crucial in considering people for supervisory, managerial, and executive jobs and in defining people's development needs.

Knowledge

Knowledge includes the technical and organizational knowledge required to do a job. This is usually the easiest component of the Success Profile to evaluate, but can be problematic in China, where fake diplomas and certificates of competence abound. Knowing the specific technical and knowledge requirements of a position can help guide managers to ask follow-up questions on activities that will help them differentiate between what a candidate shares that is real and what is not.

Job Motivation and Personal Attributes

Most Chinese hires who ultimately fail do so because of deficiencies in their personal attributes rather than their skills. Personal attributes include:

- Personal motivation
- Teamwork orientation
- Positive relationships with supervisors
- Conscientiousness
- Extroversion
- Agreeability
- Self-confidence

Motivation is a personal attribute that is important in all jobs. Hiring managers must seek information to determine if a candidate has the specific motivations required of the target position. This is particularly important if the job for which the individual is being considered is very different from his or her current position. For example, after a person has been in a technical job for several years, does he or she really want to coach and manage others, or is the person's motivation merely for the title rather than the job duties? We recently spoke with an expatriate executive who, after a reshuffling of his organization, inherited a group of five managers. As the executive had conversations with each manager about his expectations for them as leaders, he realized that only one had the propensity to lead, coach, and motivate others. The other four were promoted to the manager title based on respect for their seniority over the years as opposed to their desire to lead people.

In China, team orientation is particularly important when the new hire will be working in a group or at least working collaboratively with others. There are many new university graduates and experienced managers who work well in teams, but there also are those who are not so motivated; they're happiest working on their own.

A Success Profile for a specific job should define what is required for success in the *future* and should not automatically reprise what people in that position have done in the past to succeed. (Things change rapidly in China.) Thus, the best place to start in constructing a Success Profile is to consider how the organization's strategy intersects with a specific job's responsibilities.

Computerized programs are available that help organizations build Success Profiles.

2. Develop a Structured, Efficient Selection Process

A structured selection process (interviews, tests, targeted simulations, assessment centers, and reference checks) is needed to obtain data on the Success Profile components for the target position or job level. Selection systems are most often depicted as a series of funnels (see Figure 4.2). The process starts with recruitment at the top and ends with a hiring decision and the individual starting work at the company ("on-boarding"). An effective manager ensures that all the funnels are operating effectively.

Figure 4.2: Typical Selection Process (stars indicate desirable candidates)

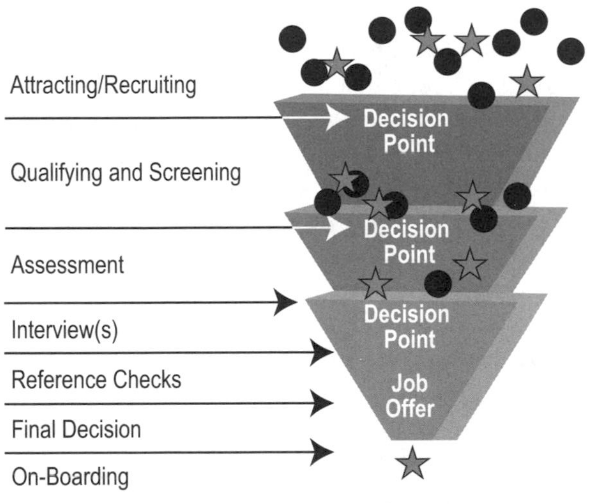

Attracting/Recruiting

Decision Point

Qualifying and Screening

Decision Point

Assessment

Decision Point

Interview(s)

Reference Checks

Job Offer

Final Decision

On-Boarding

The components of a selection process are discussed below.

Attracting/Recruiting

Organizations need to cast a wide net for candidates. The more choices, the better the final decision, but the sheer number of candidates is less important than the quality of the candidates.

Qualifying and Screening

The appropriate qualifying and prescreening of candidates often goes overlooked in China. For some jobs, well-known organizations get hundreds or even thousands of curricula vitae on paper or over the Web each week. Microsoft, for instance, has no shortage of applicants. The company receives 16,000 to 17,000 applications for 300 open positions.[2] There will be no shortage of candidates with no experience or just two to three years' experience. A December 2006 report from the government-affiliated Chinese Academy of Social Sciences projected that there would be 25 million urban job seekers chasing 10 million jobs in 2007.[3]

Because companies can't effectively interview large numbers of applicants, they need a way to sort the curricula vitae. Often, this task is given to a junior HR person or, worse, to an intern who really doesn't understand the position for which individuals are being considered and who subsequently does a poor job by passing along unqualified candidates who will waste interviewers' time; conversely, that person often misses qualified candidates who could make valuable contributions if hired. An investment in automated, online applicant screening has paid off handsomely for many large multinational companies in China. Often, the rub is that many recruitment departments enjoy their size, power, and importance in bringing talent into the organization; as a result, many are reluctant to outsource or automate the work despite the promise of improved efficiency.

Assessment

The assessment phase might include paper-and pencil tests, but more often includes simulations of the job or job level for which candidates are being considered. More and more organizations are using assessment center methodologies to literally observe individuals doing the kind of work they would do in the target job. The use of assessment centers also is described later this chapter.

Interview(s)

Almost all Chinese organizations use interviews to help make final decisions about applicants. However, these interviews often are not targeted to the most important success areas, nor are they consistent for all applicants (some may get very little time, and others may get a long interview, depending on the time pressure facing the interviewer). And, the interviewer often talks more than the interviewee. These and many more interviewer mistakes can be avoided by using the same behavior-based Targeted Selection® interviews that are used by many large organizations around the world. Targeted Selection techniques have been developed by DDI to enhance the efficiency and fairness of the interview process.[4]

Not only can Targeted Selection interviewing be used in China, but it works very well. It produces meaningful, valid information for selection and promotion decisions that can be easily interpreted and shared. Also, the system does not force interviewers to be amateur psychologists who have to analyze candidates' motivations and behaviors. In addition, Chinese candidates who have been through a well-conducted Targeted Selection interview typically report that they are impressed by the sincerity of interviewers' intentions to understand their past experiences. Rather than seeming invasive, the Targeted Selection process helps to build a rapport between the candidate and the interviewer.

What Is Behavior-Based, Targeted Selection® Interviewing?

The central premise of behavior-based interviewing is that past behavior is a reliable predictor of future behavior. Interview questions are designed to solicit information about past behavior. For example, to better understand candidates' ability in applied learning, the following questions might be asked:

> *In any new job, there are some things we pick up quickly and other things that take more time to learn. In your previous job, tell me about something you picked up quickly and something that took more time to learn. How did you go about it? What worked best, and what didn't work at all?*

> *What did you have to learn to be effective in your last job? How long did that take you? Which part took the most time? Why?*

Behavior-based interviewing was first developed in 1970 by DDI and named Targeted Selection because the questions are targeted at factors critical to job success. Targeted Selection training involves both interviewing and decision-making skills. The program has been translated into Chinese and adapted for the Chinese culture. For example, a typical Western behavioral interview practice is to ask a candidate to provide an example of ineffective handling of a situation or task. Asking a Chinese candidate to describe such an instance would not be very well received; culturally, such a request would seem odd and inappropriate, assuming it is even understood. In China the same information can be obtained in a different way.

Behavior-based interviews in China can be more difficult than many Western managers are accustomed to, because many Chinese candidates generalize excessively; others frequently digress from a question's topic. The interviewer will find it necessary to redirect candidates more often by using follow-up questions designed to solicit information about specific experiences. Interviewing managers will need to spend time coaxing out information that interviewees might not want to disclose for fear of losing face. Interviewers also will need to spend time making interviewees feel comfortable. As a result, interviews might take 60 to 90 minutes. Targeted Selection training helps managers overcome all these challenges. It is used successfully by many organizations in China for selection and promotion decisions at all organizational levels.

Reference Checks

Reference checking is particularly important in China because of the proclivity of many applicants to exaggerate their achievements. Organizations need to verify degrees and certificates by contacting the institutions that awarded them. These schools should hold records of their graduates and be able to verify the degrees and academic records.

Because fake degrees are so prevalent, some organizations use a test to evaluate minimal skills that would be expected of a graduate. If a person does not pass that test, then a special effort to verify the degree is made. An example of such a test that checks the veracity of MBA degrees is described later in this chapter.

Checking personal references is more difficult in China because people are reluctant to say anything negative about others. More often than not, reference checks are not done. If a company takes the time to do a reference check, then it is really a mere formality, as the discussion is typically on the surface with all parties remaining vague. However, accurate references can be obtained using a variation of Targeted Selection interviewing techniques. Instead of using the techniques on the applicant, they can be applied with the person who provides the reference. Individuals who must do a lot of reference checking should get special training in how to collect meaningful information. In China, accurate reference checking also depends on where you get the information. Reference checks on candidates who are applying for jobs requiring extensive external contact are less difficult because hiring managers can tap into their personal business network to get information in the field.

Probationary Periods

Probationary periods are quite common in China and should be considered part of an organization's selection system. They are particularly important because checking references is much more difficult than in the West. The best organizations use the probationary period to systematically observe employees' performance and behavior so they can make evidence-based decisions on retaining people. Failing to use a structured process to observe and evaluate employee performance during the probationary period can cost an organization a great deal of money if an individual turns out to be a poor performer after the probation expires. A labor law, passed in 2007 and effective starting in 2008, requires severance pay for termination of an employee's contract unless there is proof of severe violation of company rules.[5]

3. Hire for Job Fit Motivation and Cultural Fit Motivation in Addition to Job Skills

Job fit motivation deals with these kinds of questions:

- Is the individual motivated to do the job(s) for which he or she will be responsible?
- Does he or she get enjoyment from doing the kind of work required in the target job?
- Does the person want to be a leader or a "doer"?
- Does the person want to be out front in the organization dealing with customers or have more of a backroom role solving problems?
- Does the person want to work at a desk all day or be traveling?
- Does the person want to keep learning and be challenged, or does he or she feel learning stops with formal education?

Job fit is important in all countries and cultures, especially so in China where many individuals are so determined to get a good job in a good company that they fail to accurately consider what tasks they will be doing when they get that job. This often leads to early turnover for such individuals.

Just as important as job fit motivation is cultural fit motivation. Cultural fit addresses this question: *Will the individual fit into the organization?* For example, some people are cautious and require a great deal of information before they make a decision. Such people don't fit well in a company that is fast and dynamic. Some organizations are built around trust, sharing, and cooperation. Such a culture is attractive to some people and not to others. It's very important that the prospective organization's culture is explained to applicants so they have an opportunity, if needed, to select themselves out of consideration. But, as with job fit motivation, this is not sufficient in China; an interviewer can't just describe the organization's culture and then ask, "Would you like to work here?" Too many applicants will say yes without really considering what working in such an environment would mean. Interviewers must actively seek evidence of cultural fit during the interview.

Building prospective interviewers' skills in evaluating cultural and job fit should be part of any interview training program. Also, it might be appropriate for an organization to use job and cultural fit questionnaires to focus the interviewer's attention on potential mismatches.

Evaluating Job and Cultural Fit with a Motivation Assessment Inventory

Many Chinese organizations improve their accuracy in evaluating job and cultural fit through the use of motivation assessment inventories, which measure an individual's work-related likes and dislikes. Usually, these instruments contain straightforward questions about facets of motivation such as preference for type of pay structure, desire to work in teams, and inclination to lead people. The person's profile on these facets is compared to the profile of successful people in the target job to determine the degree of fit. Results of the comparison are then used to target interview questions to pin down the importance of the identified job or cultural preference and its likely impact on job performance.

An Example of Success

In one company where technological knowledge was the critical deciding point, 8 of 10 new hires left in their first year (6 left involuntarily because of performance and behavior issues, and 2 left voluntarily). In the first year after installing Targeted Selection and training interviewers to assess and evaluate cultural and job fit, only one individual left the organization (voluntarily, to return to school). Additionally, the organization found that the time to productivity of people hired under the new system was much faster.

4. Train Managers to Be Effective Interviewers

A company would not put a new salesperson in front of a customer without first training that individual. Similarly, managers should not be allowed to interview applicants without appropriate interviewer skills training. There are just too many skills that need to be developed. The interviewer must be able to:

- Understand the competencies that will be targeted in the interview. Too many interviewers focus on unimportant areas or only one or two competencies when, in reality, a number of competencies are important to job success.
- Recognize behavior. Many interviewers mistake applicant comments about what they would do for what they actually have done.
- Ask follow-up questions (e.g., to pin down the applicant's role in a successful sale or project).
- Manage the interview so all the targeted competencies are covered in sufficient depth to make an accurate evaluation in the time allotted.
- Maintain the applicant's self-esteem (face) so he or she feels at ease and gives truthful, open answers.

- Review the interview data accurately and evaluate each assigned target competency.

These and many other skills are taught as part of the Targeted Selection interviewer training program along with how to integrate information from multiple interviewers and data from tests, simulations, and assessment centers to make an accurate final decision.

5. Use Tests, Targeted Simulations, Assessment Centers, and Reference Checks to Supplement Interview Data

DDI has found a considerable increase in selection and promotion accuracy when supplements to interviews are provided. Research around the world has shown that the addition of tests, simulations, and especially assessment centers increases the accuracy of selection systems, particularly leadership and management selection systems.

Tests

Chinese candidates are very receptive to test instruments, in part because students in China are tested at each step in the school system. From imperial times, national tests have been used to decide who could enter the civil service.

Today, all high school students in China take university exams. Because most Chinese feel that such tests are "scientific" and fair, they willingly take them. Tests have become an accepted, integral part of the culture.

Testing instruments can predict personal attributes—such as potential for teamwork, applied learning, and customer orientation—in addition to knowledge and skill areas. Tests can be used to scale down the number of candidates to a much smaller pool so that more detailed assessment techniques—such as behavior-based Targeted Selection interviewing and simulations—can then be used.

Warning

> Many tests sold in China are simply translations of tests used in the U.S. or Europe. They have not been adapted for the Chinese culture.

> Many companies have created their own tests; however, they do so with no validation of the tests' ability to predict success at the right level.

One final bit of advice on using tests in China: Make sure that your human resources department is secure and that the staff can be relied upon not to improperly disclose the company's scoring system for its testing instruments. In a *guanxi*-obsessed society, you will often be amazed to discover who is connected to whom and how news and other information spreads despite your best efforts to contain it. For this reason and for simplicity of administration, the local HR people of many companies are not provided with the scoring algorithm. Instead, test results are e-mailed to consulting organizations that score and interpret them.

A Test to Check if MBAs Are Valid

As noted earlier, it is a common practice in China to fake university degrees. The most common bogus degree is the MBA. DDI offers a test designed to check if an applicant has acquired the minimum knowledge of an MBA graduate. Applicants who claim to hold an MBA are asked to answer a series of questions that require knowledge of the common areas covered in an MBA curriculum, such as accounting, economics, financial business strategy, human resource management, information systems, international business, marketing, operations management, public policy, and strategy.

Applicants who fail the test are then subjected to a rigorous reference check and interview to explain the poor showing.

Behavioral Simulations

Behavioral simulations are frequently used to evaluate targeted competencies in situations where an individual has not had opportunities to demonstrate such competencies in previous jobs. For example, many people who apply for sales positions in China have never had a formal sales job before, so it's not possible to ask them about former sales situations. An alternative is to give them information about a product or service and a prospective customer and then let them demonstrate how they would use their skills to convince the role-playing "customer" to buy that product or service. Applicants don't explain what they would do or say; instead, they do it! Even for those with previous experience in a job such as sales, simulations provide an opportunity to evaluate all candidates through a similar lens.

Most Chinese candidates like simulations, because they reflect the hiring company's serious intent. Being selected via such a process gives candidates face. A job offer will be treated more seriously if a simulation was included in the selection process. Simulations also provide applicants with a job preview, which helps them make better decisions about their fit with the position.

A major challenge in China is the selection of first-level leaders. Simulations are particularly effective in these situations. Even though they've never been formal leaders, many people have excellent leadership skills, which can be brought out through simulations.

A Note on Behavioral Simulations

To be effective, behavioral simulations must be carefully constructed, consistently applied, and carefully observed by trained individuals.

The most effective behavioral simulations in China mimic real-life job situations (e.g., selling a product or an idea, handling an unhappy customer, dealing with an employee who consistently arrives late, providing feedback to an underperforming individual). These simulations usually take less than 15 minutes and can be inserted into a Targeted Selection interview to get insights that would be otherwise unobtainable through the interview process.

Most common behavioral simulations work well in China. But there is one exception: leaderless group discussions in which participants are expected to openly debate an issue within the group. Putting forward your ideas and challenging others in this type of group situation runs counter to traditional Chinese culture; such simulation discussions are likely to fall flat in China.

Assessment Centers

Assessment centers are larger-scale simulations of the critical components of a leadership position for which an individual is being considered. Assessment centers have three primary uses in China:

- Determine the leadership and managerial potential of university graduates who are being considered for a fast-track development program.
- Aid in making key managerial and executive hiring or placement decisions.
- Identify the development needs of individuals in middle- and upper-management positions.

The length and sophistication of the centers depend on their purpose and the job (or job level) simulated. Half-day assessment centers for selecting supervisors and lower-level management can be offered at a consultant's facility or can be set up at a company location. They rely heavily on phone, rather than face-to-face, interactions.

A special type of assessment center designed to select high-level managers and executives and/or define their development areas is the one-day Acceleration Center® (see the following sidebar). Acceleration Centers®, provided by DDI, take place in a special facility where e-mail and voice mail communications are simulated and the interactions of role-play participants are recorded on video.

Acceleration Centers are more high-level, more elaborate assessment centers that feature a unique "day-in-the-life" simulation for executives and can be used to speed their development. DDI offers Acceleration Centers in Beijing, Shanghai, Hong Kong, Taipei, and Singapore as well as many other major cities throughout the world.

Assessment centers in general are becoming very popular among progressive companies in China, because they provide critical, independent insights to aid important hiring, placement, and development decisions. They function outside of normal organizational pressures (e.g., pressure to promote someone because the person has been on the job for three years or is the cousin of an important government official).

Assessment centers are popular with candidates because they are perceived as fair and an investment by the company in their career. The relationship between a properly designed and executed assessment center and the job is obvious, which makes people believe in the assessment center's accuracy. Individuals who participate feel they have had a fair chance to show the company what they can do.

A Day in the Life of an Acceleration Center® Participant

Acceleration Centers allow participants to try on senior roles, accountabilities, and responsibilities in a relatively risk-free, simulated environment. Participants usually find that these "stretch" experiences deliver important self-insights and give them a realistic job preview. Here's an example, as seen through the eyes of a participating manager:

If you're being perfectly honest with yourself, you're a little nervous— perhaps more than a little. You've visited your new company's web site and found out all about the ABC Corporation. You've read that you're a new vice president and that you and the CEO are traveling and unavailable for the next few days. It's 8 a.m.; you face a dizzying collection of e-mails and voice mails that demand replies. If that weren't enough, you have a very full schedule of meetings, and your boss needs a strategic plan by the end of the day.

Welcome to the deep end of the pool!

> *You dig in, establishing priorities for everything and organizing your time. You meet with Dana Wright, a peer who is upset about one of your staff—and who once held the job you hold now.*

> *You get three more e-mails.*

> *You meet with an irate customer who's ready to jump ship.*

> *You get four more e-mails.*

> *You meet with Wang Xu, who's been late filing government forms for your company's make-or-break new product.*

> *You have a working lunch to begin creating your strategic plan.*

> *You meet with Ron Jackson, whose company could be a profitable strategic partner. But now Ron wants to buy your company's technology outright.*

> *You review new e-mail and voice mail messages.*

> *You do a live interview with a local television reporter who has heard rumors that health hazards might be linked to your products and is digging for an exposé.*

> *You add some final touches to your strategic plan, which you will present to a group of vice presidents. And you review your speech, which you hope will motivate and inspire a heretofore lackluster workforce.*

> *Your presentation and speech, except for a few minor glitches, go better than expected. It's around 6 p.m., and the whirlwind is over. You've made it through!*

It's been a demanding 10 hours. You've solved strategic problems, tested your vision, and addressed vendor problems, personnel matters, and professional jealousies. You've smoothed ruffled feathers, averted disasters, built trust, demonstrated leadership, delegated, and established a strategic direction. You feel tired, but good.

The deep end of the pool isn't so bad after all.

6. Train Managers to Make Accurate Hiring Decisions Using All Available Information

The 2005 DDI survey, *Leadership in China: Keeping Pace with a Growing Economy,* concluded that nearly half the surveyed managers in China had poor or fair hiring skills, meaning that they don't make the best hiring decisions. Of course, part of their problem is the lack of appropriate tools (i.e., tests, simulations, interviews), but it also reflects the lack of a systematic decision-making process. As the study found, very few Chinese managers are highly skilled at sharing and integrating behavioral data; this is a major growth opportunity for most Chinese organizations.[6]

Effective selection decisions have the following characteristics:
- More than one manager is involved in the hiring decision. Three seems to be an optimal number.
- Managers share interview data around the target competencies or other Success Profile areas. For example, if two managers interviewed a candidate for planning skills, each would share what was learned with the other. If a technical test was administered, the data would be used by the managers when discussing that technical area.
- During the discussion, managers question each other to be sure they understand the data presented. Then they agree on a rating for each competency.
- Finally, the managers consider all the data on an individual and make an appropriate decision.

The big advantage of this more systematic, structured decision-making process is that it forces managers to think through all the areas that are important to the job and not be overly influenced by a candidate's particularly good English-speaking skills, university accreditations, or other apparent strengths. It delays a decision until all the data are in and understood by all managers. And, because the decision-making process involves more than one person, it usually results in better hiring decisions.

HR People Are Not Necessarily Good Interviewers

In Western countries it is probably a good bet that HR representatives are trained, skilled interviewers; this, however, often is not the case in China. Many HR people have done hundreds or even thousands of interviews but still are quite inaccurate in spotting qualified or unqualified people. It is often not their fault; many are self-taught and have learned some very poor techniques and strategies along the way.

Companies in China are strongly advised to check out the interviewing skills of their key HR people by setting up situations where they can be observed interviewing a candidate in English.

Many HR people also have learned some bad lessons in how to share data among several interviewers to make a final selection decision. They might make comments such as, "He looks good to me; what do you think?" rather than systematically obtaining data on each target competency before making a final consensus decision.

7. Set Up a System to Monitor Adherence to the Selection Process and the Organization's Selection Standards

Expatriate managers need to be persistent in guarding the door to ensure that only the "right" people get on their team. When your people sing the praises of a certain potential candidate, press them for reasons why this person is so good. Ask for the individual's evaluations on each part of the Success Profile.

It is important that organizations have a well-thought-out selection process and that it is followed rigorously. Too often, interviewers and managers skip portions of a selection system and, thus, miss learning about important candidate characteristics that can lead to failure after the individual is hired.

When hiring quotas increase, it also is common in China for organizations to lower their requirement that all interviewers be trained. That is exactly the wrong time to lower interviewing standards. Rather, effective organizations put their people through even more training. They run refresher courses on interviewing and decision making to reinforce the importance of effective skills.

Some Other Considerations for Hiring in China

Coordinate Your Hiring Efforts

It pays to ensure that your organization's hiring efforts in China are coordinated and not split across divisions or business units. Getting good staff in China is difficult enough without facing competition from another division of your own company.

Consider the case of one company that was growing its business through several different channels. Two business units were seeking to hire an HR director. Because the selection processes were independent of each other, the same person became the top choice of both units. The candidate accepted one position before the other unit had a chance to make its offer. When the second offer came through, the candidate was surprised, knowing that both were from the same parent company. This placed the candidate in an awkward position: She preferred the second offer to the first. When the second business unit heard that she had already accepted the earlier offer, it promised to go to the head office to fight for her. This took time—negotiations took place and internal energy was spent working out a solution. Finally, the candidate was contacted to sort out the details. But it was too late—she had accepted another offer from a competitor. The reason for her decision? She had become too embarrassed by the situation and felt it best simply to move on.

Use Every Opportunity to Make a Positive Impression

An organization's selection system has two functions: 1) decide whom to hire, and 2) make a positive impression so that the most qualified candidate accepts the job offer. The latter is often neglected, particularly in the high-stress, high-volume hiring situation typically found in China. Yet, impression management is probably more important in China than anywhere else. After all, many Chinese are particularly interested in the brand and culture offered by an organization. The best companies determine the key areas they want to convey to applicants and assign specific areas for different interviewers to cover during their candidate interactions. For example, one interviewer might discuss training opportunities, while another might talk about the company culture. If the communication to the applicant is not organized, then the organization runs the risk that all interviewers touch on the same areas while other important areas are left uncovered.

DDI trains interviewers to use stories to describe an organization's job outlook, culture, training, development opportunities, etc. It is one thing to tell an applicant that those opportunities exist; it is quite another—and much more effective—to tell a story about how those opportunities have benefited someone in a position similar to the one the applicant is seeking.

The efficiency of the selection process also is important. Does the receptionist expect the person when he or she comes in for the interview? Are the interviewers prepared? If there is time between a selection interview and the job offer, does anyone call to check on the applicant and explain the delay?

Perhaps the best way to make an impression is to allow the applicant to spend considerable time with the leader to whom he or she would report. This will impress the individual and provide time to explore specific issues of importance. Many organizations provide only very short periods for such interactions, if they are provided at all; a company that devotes more time for a leader and an applicant to interact will automatically make a better impression. After all, young Chinese graduates are choosing a manager just as much as they are choosing a company.

Don't Overpromise in the Selection Process

It's not uncommon for managers to promise more than the organization can deliver in an effort to convince desired candidates to come on board. But be warned—such a strategy is a recipe for high turnover in the current context of China's competitive labor market.

Just as organizations plan the assessment of candidates, they should organize the description of the target job and the company culture. Although at times this task is delegated to the HR department, often it is handled by the hiring manager. Such a discussion should cover these topics:

- **Training**—The training program for new employees should be spelled out. Remember that in the Corporate Leadership Council survey, 47 percent of respondents rated internal education as a priority in selecting their job. Also, to young Chinese, "training" means formal, classroom-based training. Informal and on-the-job training are important, but are not considered actual "training." It is therefore necessary to spell out what training will be classroom based and what will be provided through mentoring or coaching.

- **Overseas training**—Is there overseas training in the first year of employment? Tell prospective employees about it, what the qualifications for such training will be, and what level of performance must be met. Overseas training will be a very strong incentive for most young candidates. If there's no overseas training or only a remote chance of it, then make this clear. There's no point in having people join a company only to leave because their expectations have gone unmet.

- **Pay raise at the end of a probationary period**—Will there be a salary increase after the individual has made it through the probationary period? State this up front, either way. (See Chapter 10 for more on probationary periods.)

- **Job title**—Starting job titles are important to candidates, but they become even more so six months or a year later, whenever they start comparing titles with their former classmates. Tell candidates whether they can expect a title promotion and, if so, under what performance criteria.

- **Company culture**—Explain the organization's culture to prospective employees, but be careful—it's very easy for applicants to misunderstand comments about culture. For example, if high-performing employees are encouraged to be "entrepreneurial," you will need to discuss what that actually means. In China, being entrepreneurial means starting your own business. You will need to give clear, real-life examples of how concepts like "entrepreneurial" specifically apply in your organization.

  Concepts like "open communication" also need to be explained. Candidates must know that it is acceptable to ask for help when there are difficulties or barriers and that their leaders need to be told everything— not just the good news. Candidates also need to know they are expected to contribute outside the scope of their job description, if that is true in your organization.

  In some situations it is also important to explain the extent to which individuals' day-to-day job performance will be monitored. If so, explain the reason for the monitoring; otherwise, it will be interpreted as mistrust.

- **How to get the next job grade/position**—Chinese employees commonly have the misperception that learning and working hard will guarantee success (i.e., promotion). While both obviously are important in determining an individual's prospects for promotion, so too are being productive, achieving desired outcomes, and maintaining appropriate relationships with coworkers and supervisors. Be sure candidates understand this.

Also, explain what candidates can reasonably hope for in terms of promotional opportunities. Surveys suggest that fresh graduates want to reach management level within three years of graduation. If this is not realistic at your organization, then that must be made clear and prospective employees should be told what can be accomplished within three years.

Many organizations do a poor job of communicating their culture. They know they should provide appropriate explanations in order to reduce or prevent turnover, but they either forget to do it (often because the task is not specifically assigned) or fail to do it for fear of losing the applicant. To ensure appropriate communication of their culture, organizations need to plan what must be covered and designate a person to make it part of their interaction with applicants.

Other Thoughts About Selection System Implementations

- Increasingly, foreign companies in China are outsourcing some or all of their hiring processes to HR consultants. When this happens, it's important that the selection process is completely customized to the specific Success Profiles for the jobs being filled. Typically, expatriate managers will want to make the final hiring decision, but local managers often ask HR consultants to make it. Why? Because it allows the Chinese managers to mitigate the risk of making a difficult decision. If the new hire fails, then the consultants can be blamed. Ensure that your managers take responsibility for their hiring decisions.

- With the shortage of good local managers, some foreign companies in China recruit ethnic Chinese managers and professionals from outside mainland China—from Hong Kong, Taiwan, Southeast Asia, and perhaps from North America, the United Kingdom, or Australia. Many are well educated and often can speak fluent Mandarin and English.

  At first glance, such a strategy appears ideal. But companies have found that many of the Chinese they recruit from Hong Kong, for example, leave within a relatively short time to pursue their own entrepreneurial ventures in China. Careful selection is needed.

- Another problem with non-mainland Chinese employees can be that although they look Chinese, as far as the locals are concerned they don't think and operate like Chinese. Resentment and cultural confusion can build up on both sides. Many of these ethnic Chinese will experience the same frustrations that beset other Western managers in China. But on top of those, these leaders will have to face difficulties that arise from the contradictions between their Chinese appearance and their lack of Chinese thinking. Companies often find that their expectations of such recruits are unrealistically high.

- Also, the Chinese-language skills of non-mainland Chinese often are not as good as might be assumed. In 2007 Goldman Sachs Group ran into problems when it wanted to promote its co-head of Asia investment banking to CEO of its China securities joint venture. Their plans were dashed when the would-be CEO could not write Chinese well enough to take a government test required of all new senior managers at local securities firms. The individual in question was ethnically Chinese, from Malaysia. Although he spoke fluent Chinese, his Chinese writing was relatively poor. A mainland Chinese with the requisite Chinese language and writing skills had to be promoted instead.[7]

- The so-called "returnees" comprise another potentially rich source of leadership talent. This group is part of the "brain drain" that left China in search of better opportunities than the mainland could offer. Many are being tempted back. Like the Hong Kong recruits, they seem to provide the ideal mix of management skills and Chinese-language skills. But again, many leave to start their own companies once they have made sufficient contacts. And again, the best remedy is a good, well-executed selection system.

- Remember, it's difficult to replace poor performers in China because of cultural and legal reasons—labor tribunals typically side with employees.

Get It Right

Selecting your team or new members is one of the most important tasks any expatriate manager will have in China. The difference between getting it right and the alternative ultimately will determine your company's ability to compete in China. But selecting your team is very much only the end of the beginning when it comes to leadership challenges in China. The complexities of managing and coaching your team and growing your own leaders should not be underestimated; in fact, these topics comprise the focus for the remainder of this book. Once you have a team, the most fundamental task will be to establish trust with its individual members. This is key to building a successful team and is the theme of the next chapter.

第5章

CHAPTER 5

The Essential Nature of Trust

"Followership is trust," said Peter Drucker.[1] Nowhere is that more true than in China, where trust is the cornerstone of all relationships. Without trust there can be no relationship—certainly not one that is meaningful or that will prove constructive. It's your responsibility as a leader to make a conscious effort to build trust. "Build" is the operative word here, because trust cannot be demanded; rather, it is granted and it is earned—and it takes time.

So, how do you earn trust in China? You can start by avoiding the traps that erode trust among your China staff and turn it into mistrust.

What Expatriate Managers Do to Create Mistrust

No expatriate manager deliberately sets out to create mistrust between him- or herself and the local staff. But some actions these managers take or decisions they make often unwittingly break down trust. Many of these behaviors can be avoided. For example, when decisions seem inconsistent, trust will suffer. When expatriate leaders become too cliquish, local employees get suspicious, thinking that some closed-door agreement—informal or otherwise—is excluding them from decisions being made about them. If this happens, no longer will there be one team, but two—the expatriate managers and the locals. This is one of the easiest trust traps into which expatriates can fall.

Here are some examples of trust traps:

- At the end of a meeting, the CEO asks the expatriate staff to stay behind for a discussion. All local managers leave the meeting room first. The expatriate team discusses "critical issues," leading to decisions that are announced without input from the local team. How will the local managers perceive this? Most likely, they will feel that when it comes to decision making, their input simply isn't valued.

- Expatriate leaders frequent a particular corner or table in the cafeteria, but without the local managers, who assume the expatriates are not interested in establishing personal relationships with them.

- When an expatriate leaves an assignment, the vacant position is not opened to all applicants. Instead, another expatriate is quickly named to fill the vacancy. The local managers are likely to assume the selection was based on "nationality" rather than competency.

- During a meeting the expatriate manager explains to the local team that "this is how we do this at home" (or in the home office) without any other justification and that the locals must follow the same practice. Local managers might see this as arrogant, with the expatriate being unwilling to understand the local situation.

- A young (27- or 28-year-old) expatriate manager is sent to fill a job and is seen as not having much experience. Local managers are likely to perceive the company as unfair—that it selects people based on nationality and perhaps their connections rather than their competence. A perception that the company is unwilling to develop local staff might arise.

A Trust Trap Triggered by an Expatriate Manager

Wen Bin Chen is the director of engineering and one of the few Chinese on the company's China operations management team.

One morning Wen Bin meets Ralph, the general manager, in the elevator. Ralph joined the China operations a year ago.

Ralph smiles at Wen Bin and says, "Last year, we had to cancel several of our overseas training programs for our staff. But these programs are important, and now that our sales are better, we need to make them up this year." He then asks Wen Bin to present his ideas for staff training at the budget meeting the next day.

A few hours later, Wen Bin asks his key staff to join him for lunch to discuss their needs and ideas about training. He takes their ideas into consideration in crafting his plan, which he presents at the meeting the next day. But at the meeting, Ralph is not so receptive and says, "Our sales are improving, but we're not profitable yet. Why are you thinking of sending so many people overseas for training? Sending a few would be OK, but not 20!"

Wen Bin doesn't argue; he knows from experience that to do so would be pointless. But he can't help but think to himself, "You asked me for a training plan, but now you've changed your position and embarrassed me in front of my coworkers and direct reports."

Wen Bin feels he has lost face. He will not be so trusting of Ralph in the future, and he feels that a little more distance between himself and Ralph might now be best.

Change itself presents a breeding ground for mistrust. Organizations often redirect their strategies and priorities and stop funding certain initiatives for various reasons. These kinds of changes can be easily misunderstood by Chinese employees, who might see a budget cut as a personal affront. The secret, of course, is to fully communicate the reasons and the situation.

Inconsistency is another trust trap. If a manager behaves differently at different times, then the team will spend much of its time trying to figure out what the boss wants rather than what's right for the organization. Sometimes leaders are inconsistent because they lack conviction. Chinese employees want and need managers they can respect, not managers who are weak and tend to lean in the direction everyone else seems to be leaning.

On many occasions managers will be approached by their people for unwarranted benefits or privileges. It's important to stand firm in refusing to grant such requests; otherwise, rumors of favoritism will spread and mistrust will emerge. Some new expatriate managers try to earn their staff's acceptance by granting requests and favors, but such practices tend to sow perceptions of unfairness and, over time, when it seems prudent to no longer grant such favors, a perception of inconsistency also will creep in. The paramount need is to be seen as a fair leader, not an easy one.

Similarly, bad news needs to be accepted graciously. Many expatriate managers tend to react adversely—perhaps visibly or vocally—to bad news. While this might be an acceptable practice in the West, local staff often will perceive this as a reaction to them personally and feel they are being blamed. They might lose face even though they are merely acting as the messenger. Such a reaction from their manager will make them and their colleagues reluctant in the future to share bad news. In turn, this will lead to delays in reporting such news, and that will further exacerbate the feelings of mistrust. Many expatriates in China report that they constantly feel that they never really know what is going on in the office. This is one of the reasons why.

The Cultural Setting as a Source of Mistrust

Chinese communication style is diffuse, not specific. This can create an impression that individuals are unwilling to share information. Typically in conversations, Chinese start with a general point and move to specifics only if prompted to do so. But without a prompt, the conversation is unlikely to go beyond the general. The Chinese will be satisfied with such a discussion because all was in accordance with established social etiquette; the unenlightened Westerner, however, will wonder what the point of the conversation was.

All of this can create the impression to the expatriate that the local Chinese are obfuscating or being unclear or inscrutable, perhaps even willfully so. Trust can break down because of such cultural miscues.

Still other aspects of China—such as the complexities of government bureaucracy and how officials are ranked—never will be fully understood by most foreigners. Even local employees, who have experience in dealing with this kind of ambiguity, have to "feel" their way around certain situations each time. This is one reason they might not be able to give precise answers about how long approvals and clearances might take. Communist Party membership is difficult to explain to the outsider. Many Party members join at an early age, and it can be politically difficult or unwise to end that membership voluntarily. Although they maintain their membership, many members are not active in the Party.

To gain further awareness of possible trust traps, expatriates must remain open to how a culture, its people, or a distinct generation might collectively think. By leveraging this awareness for a more comprehensive understanding of the local talent, the expatriate can, in turn, reduce a potential source of mistrust.

Remaining Open to Different Perspectives

An expatriate CFO of a German engineering company had to terminate a long-time project manager because he was awarding bids to a company in which he was the director and part owner. This was not a shock to the CFO as it was not the first time he had encountered this type of unethical behavior. But the real surprise was his team's response to the situation. The team did not comment on how unethical the individual was; instead, they unanimously felt the individual was foolish for being so brazen as to list himself as the company's director. They went on to share with the CFO that the individual should have used the name of a relative as his company's director—just as so many others do. The CFO was open to hearing their perspective and noted their comments. Then he went on to explain why the rules were enforced and their long-term importance for the good of the company.

What Local Employees Do to Cause Mistrust

Trust is not a one-way street. Local employees have the potential to lose the trust of expatriate managers too. China's unique environment and culture help to create communication and perception gaps that trigger trust traps. The following scenarios show how some of these traps might arise.

SCENARIO 1

Weiwei is responsible for customs clearances in the import and export department. She knows she is under scrutiny because in order for the production line in her company to start on time, the necessary equipment must first be cleared through customs.

Lillian, Weiwei's manager and an expatriate leader, reviews the customs status each morning with her and routinely asks when the clearances will be given. Weiwei's best answer always is, "I will try."

Lillian is from Hong Kong. Although she speaks Mandarin, she knows that government relations are best handled by local people. Nonetheless, she is becoming increasingly frustrated with Weiwei, who seems unable or unwilling to say when the equipment will be cleared through customs.

From Weiwei's experience, government bureaucracy is unpredictable. She has good connections with the customs officials, but she cannot guarantee when all the paperwork will be approved. Nor does she feel that she can follow up with the customs office every day, because that will simply annoy them.

From Weiwei's perspective, her manager is a typical expatriate who doesn't understand *guo qing*—how things are done in China—despite Lillian being an ethnic Chinese herself.

Scenario 2

Elizabeth is the human resource director of a start-up operation. An expatriate manager, she will return to her home country in two years, a detail that she has made clear to her local team.

When recruiting her team, Elizabeth selected at least two candidates who might have the potential to assume her position when she leaves China.

Connie Yen is one of Elizabeth's potential successors. She has the right experience, having worked for an international company in which she was promoted to senior HR manager after eight years. A headhunting firm then recruited Connie into her current position. Although she was not looking to change jobs, the challenge of working at a start-up appealed to her.

Connie has proven to be a competent manager. She has solid operational and technical skills and is a good people manager. She has demonstrated good coaching skills with her team, and her communication skills are excellent. Elizabeth consults Connie on all important decisions and values her advice on strategic and operational issues.

All went well until the third month of Elizabeth's stint. She learned that by law, all companies must allow employees who are Communist Party members to hold regular meetings if the Party members desire it. Soon after, when Elizabeth heard that Connie is a Party member, she asked Connie to come to her office.

"I've heard that you are a Communist Party member. Is that true?" asks Elizabeth.

"I thought of telling you," replies Connie, "but I didn't think it related to my work here, so I didn't."

Elizabeth does not say anything, but she would have preferred that Connie had told her earlier. Now she wonders if there is anything else about Connie that she should know.

SCENARIO 3

All has been going well at Company X's China operations, which has recently expanded its staff to more than 1,000. The local labor authority informs the China branch that it is time for it to establish a labor union. Local law requires larger companies to have a union; furthermore, 2 percent of the payroll must be submitted to the central union authority.

The expatriate managers are concerned about the implications. Xiaoping, the local HR manager, explains to Richard, the expatriate regional HR director, that unions in China today function more as welfare organizations for the employees. Although Xiaoping doesn't say so, Richard suspects the fees are probably the real reason that the local authority is urging the formation of a union.

Richard is annoyed. Why hadn't Xiaoping alerted him to the union issue before? "The head office is sensitive to unions," he tells Xiaoping. "I can't tell them tomorrow that we need a union and then set it up next week. We need to show evidence that this is a requirement in China and that a union can be managed in a way that will not threaten the company." Richard is raising his voice without realizing it.

Richard thinks to himself that the locals are not totally reliable for sharing information. Unions are a sensitive matter to the head office, and if he can't handle this matter well, it might have a negative impact on his chances for promotion.

But now Xiaoping is annoyed as well. "I did not know this was so sensitive," he says. "You did not tell me. . . . Other foreign companies set up unions. This is the norm in China!" He also wonders why Richard is angry and seems to be blaming him. "The union issue is out of my control. I didn't think I needed to tell you about this," he says. Both men now feel that the other has failed to keep the other informed.

Political and Organizational Differences as a Source of Mistrust

Many Chinese employees lack organizational and political acumen regarding issues that are sensitive to Western organizations. Unions are a good example. They are unexceptional in socialist economies such as China's and have not played much of a role since the economy opened up. But for ideological reasons, the government will not diminish their standing. Chinese employees have come to see unions as integral to working for a major company, even if the unions are not particularly active. As a result, many Chinese do not understand Western apprehension about unionization. This is a prime example of a topic that expatriate managers need to discuss with their local staffs so that the locals will understand Western political perceptions and sensitivities.

Additionally, expatriates need to educate their Chinese employees about who should be copied on e-mails and proposals, what should be included on formal meeting agendas, what should be put in writing, what should never be recorded in this way, etc. It is the manager's responsibility to identify and close such perception and communication gaps. Organizational practices that are understood in the West cannot be similarly assumed in China.

How to Build Trust

Trust can be earned; it cannot be demanded. Given that the process of building trust takes time, it's best to get started right away. Following are several trust-building strategies.

Instill the Practice of Communicating Upward

Expatriate managers often complain that local employees hide information or problems from them, because they do not volunteer information. This is a problem of immense importance in China. To be sure, there is no easy solution. Any remedy involves overcoming an aspect of traditional Chinese culture that is deeply ingrained. As an expatriate manager, you will need to invest some time. Try spending more time talking one on one with each employee. After a formal meeting is usually a good time to talk with a select individual. If it turns out that the person has some concerns and didn't express them to the group, ask him or her, in confidence, to explain why. If the individual is willing to share those concerns with you in private, this will be a significant step in building trust.

Employees need to be reassured that if they disclose sensitive information or alert you to problems, they will neither suffer consequences nor be revealed as a source of the information. It's also important that managers treat mistakes as learning opportunities. The balance between maintaining high performance standards and tolerating learning from errors is always a dilemma for managers.

When courting feedback, opinions, or any other type of upward information sharing, be careful to listen to different perspectives. Avoid becoming captive of one or a few direct reports simply because they have good English skills or are especially empathetic; otherwise, you risk creating a perception of favoritism.

Solicit Feedback on Your Leadership Style

Soliciting feedback is a very Western concept. Unless you are in China for an extended period or develop some very close personal relationship there, you will find getting candid feedback from Chinese employees to be very difficult; they simply are not open about their views of their leaders. If you are sensitive enough, you might be able to detect some feedback, but the signals will be weak. Instead, the real value of asking employees for their feedback might lie in the time and effort you put forth to get it. Employees will respect your effort; it will help build your relationship with them. Without sufficient quality feedback, it will be difficult for you to know how you are performing as a leader—what is working and what is not. It will be even more difficult to gauge the degree to which you have earned your staff's trust. In any event, be very careful of any information you receive.

Another method of getting this feedback is to use what are known as "multirater" or "360-degree" surveys and interviews. These involve gathering information on leadership competencies from the people—your boss, peers, and direct reports—who work with you to seek their feedback. Your self-perceptions can be compared with the perceptions of those who work with and for you. Multirater instruments can assess a range of perceptions, including those related to trust.

However, such instruments need careful adjustment to account for the Chinese cultural context. It is best that a consultant or some other trained external party administers the surveys and interviews. This will help to convince employees that the sources of the feedback will remain confidential. The third-party administrator needs to have sufficient China experience to ensure that cultural nuances will be addressed.

Numerical ratings must be interpreted carefully too. When asked to rate various competencies on a scale of, say, 1 to 5, respondents everywhere else tend to centralize their responses (i.e., turn in a rating of 3). But in China there's a tendency to centralize at a higher rating: say, 4 or 4.5. This means that relative—rather than absolute—scores must be analyzed. Write-in comments can provide further clues as to how much trust the staff has in their manager.

Develop and Communicate Team Rules

Clear guidance on "team rules" and ethics also is essential for promoting trust. You can arrive at team rules in a participatory way through a series of group discussions in which the team collectively agrees on what specific behaviors or ground rules should apply in their work environment.

Possible Elements of a Social or Team Contract

While most teams in China operate under informal rules that are understood or communicated verbally, some Western managers have facilitated the development of a more formal team contract that specifies rules like these:

> Meeting customer needs is the number one priority (quality, time, and cost are important).

> Problems will be raised openly—they are not to surface later as back-channel discussions or hallway mutterings.

> Once decisions are made in meetings, they are to be implemented as envisioned at the meetings.

> Everyone has an equal say in meetings.

> No one is to interrupt another person when he or she is speaking—all participants should be made to feel that their contributions are valued.

At the very least, development of a team contract is a means of starting a discussion of important issues.

Leaders establish trust by taking actions that are consistent with the team rules. Inconsistency and hypocrisy erode trust.

Clearly Communicate Ethical Standards

For effective enforcement of ethics in China, two things must happen:

- The ethics code must be as clear as possible, well documented, well communicated to employees at their orientation, and reinforced at subsequent meetings.
- Leaders must model the ethics. When leaders are seen to observe even the small rules, they will win the respect and trust of their direct reports. In a region where people are accustomed to seeing those who frame laws not feeling bound by them, such behavior will be very quickly noticed and appreciated.

Following are some high-level examples of rules that many organizations institute. (Obviously, to help your Chinese employees understand these rules, you would need to provide detailed specifics, limiting gray areas of interpretation.)

- Refrain from using company resources for personal purposes. For example, do not use your driver or secretary to run personal errands.
- Refuse to accept forged or faked paperwork—no matter how trifling and expected—because faked receipts abound in China.
- Differentiate work entertainment from personal entertainment.
- Exercise moderation when it comes to entertainment expenses.
- Be economical with company assets and resources.

Take a Chance with Your People

"If you don't trust the other person, don't deploy him. If you decide to deploy him, trust him." So goes a common maxim in China. It suggests that the first step an expatriate manager should take to earn the trust of his or her local staff is to trust them. Take small risks with your team by stretching their tasks, gauging the response, and then building on it.

Remember that while there is always some degree of confusion between people of different cultures (cultural miscues and so on), the incidences of willful intent are far rarer than might be believed. It takes time and patience for people from different cultures and backgrounds to align their expectations. So, be prepared to invest the time to build trust with your team and avoid any trust derailers along the way.

And If There's Little Trust?

If trust is missing, then little will be accomplished. Certainly, the work environment will not be happy, and your team will under-perform. Some might even go into sabotage mode. Ultimately, the best staff will leave, and you'll be left with more and more work to do yourself. Increasingly, you'll spend time checking up on other people's work and micromanaging. The less faith and confidence you express and demonstrate in your staff, the less they will trust you. The assumption of low trust will become a self-fulfilling prophecy.

Gaining trust is the foundation of leadership. When you put your trust in others, you are sending a strong message that says, "I respect you, and I think you are trustworthy." This tells people that you have faith in their ability and competence, and that you believe they have what it takes to do the job. Once broken, trust is seldom restored. It is the most fragile, yet essential, attribute of leadership. And that is nowhere more true than in China.

CHAPTER 6

Setting the Direction for Your China Team

Few people want to commit to a journey without first knowing the route and end destination. Your Chinese reports are no different. This chapter discusses how to provide direction for your Chinese staff and how to align their efforts with your business strategy. If you are a senior manager, that means developing a company vision and strategy and making sure they are communicated and followed. If you manage a department or functional unit, you'll need to do the same thing—first by communicating the big picture for the organization and then by explaining how your unit's strategy fits into that big picture. In other words, you need a sub-strategy that fits into the overall company strategy and ensures that your Chinese employees' objectives are aligned to it. Identifying where your staff members fit into their unit's structure and direction as well as where your unit fits into the overall corporate direction is essential for you to be able to communicate their role and relevance and to motivate them.

Moving Fast

When a new leader arrives, everyone wants to know all they can about the person as soon as possible—particularly about the organization's direction, how things are going to change, and any new reporting relationships. Young Chinese employees are ambitious; they care very much about the company's and team's direction, if only for their own self-interest. First and foremost, they are pragmatists; they care whether their leader has a clear path for the next three to five years that can support their personal career advancement.

Unfortunately, most new expatriate managers can't answer these questions. Ideally, they'd like to spend six months getting to know the job and the organization as well as understanding the operational realities in China and the market's uniqueness before committing to a new direction. So, right away there's a disconnect: Employees want to know the new direction and how their roles and behaviors need to change, while the new expatriate needs time to figure things out.

Many times the basic organizational structure and direction are already defined and won't change—at least in the short term. If this is so, then an expatriate manager is well advised to disclose that and then start working to devise sub-strategies around the periphery of the main organization strategy.

If, in fact, you (the expatriate manager) are being brought in to shake things up, reorganize, cut, or expand the workforce, then by all means, you need to get going on devising your direction and strategy. But don't take six months! In general, it's better to state a strategy and then change it, if necessary, than it is to keep everyone in limbo for an extended period of time.

Stage 1: Find Out How Things Really Operate

The first step in setting clear direction is to involve the senior people reporting to you. They will be able to contribute their knowledge, vision, and insights and help you interpret available data about the market, competition, and the like. This step is critical because it encourages these key individuals to share ownership of the process and the outcome.

It is important to develop a vision rather than a dream—a vision is grounded in current and future marketplace realities. To do this, gather information from those who have good local knowledge (such as your team, customers, and suppliers), and then assess the available and potential resources to see how far you and your team can go.

Assessing internal issues can be more difficult than assessing external ones. All participants involved in the task will be stakeholders. Each will have something to win or lose from any decisions made, so no views will be free from bias. You can expect some issues to be hidden, particularly those that might be unpleasant. Because Chinese always prefer harmony over discord, bad news rarely travels up; be aware that some *critical* issues might be hidden or glossed over.

So what techniques can be used in China to reveal all the information you need? The following approaches that have proven effective in the West also work in China.

Determine the Actual Power Arrangement

First look at the organization chart in your office and then figure out the power relationships. Hierarchy is important in China, but within that setup will be an array of other power relationships—both formal and informal. Formal relationships will include the Communist Party ranking in your company, particularly if you work in a joint venture setting. A local Party vice president might be reporting to a local manager who is younger. But outside the company—and informally, probably, inside as well—it will be the Party vice president who is the more senior. Your awareness of such relationships is key to determining who knows what and who has influence.

Do an Information Audit of Your Team

Expatriate managers need to quickly identify who knows what among their team members. Some might have excellent contacts with relevant government bodies; others might have a good understanding of China's tax system or its labor laws; still others might be experts in your local competitors' strategies. Expatriate managers sometimes need to coax this information from their staff, some of whom may be reluctant to reveal their knowledge to their colleagues. They'd rather squirrel it away for their own use rather than share it because, in their view, it would give their colleagues an advantage.

Hold One-on-One Meetings with Key Individuals

Identify key influencers and meet with them to get their insights and views. In these private sessions they will be much more willing to share what they know and can do. Finally, the one-on-one meetings can help them understand the importance of bringing issues or problems to the surface and resolving them for the good of both the company and themselves. The meetings also will allow you to better understand your key individuals' mind-sets, values, key skills, and shortfalls.

Start to Use Meetings to Solve Problems

When you feel you have a good understanding of the dynamics, shared interests, and conflicts across the organization's broader groups, bring the key stakeholders into smaller group meetings. Get them into joint problem-solving mode—have them rank and prioritize the business issues the organization faces and get them to discuss what can be done. Be aware, though, that the typical local Chinese answer to many problems is "Send us to more training." But encourage them to think about other solutions, such as how to create better accountability, reward systems, and tracking and monitoring systems.

In group meetings where you are attempting to understand the "lay of the land," ask follow-up questions to pin down information on people's views. Once trust begins to grow with your key stakeholders, ask increasingly tougher questions about problems that might arise. Delve evermore deeply into each issue while maintaining or enhancing people's self-esteem (face). When discussing solutions, push for answers that are beyond the superficial. When it comes to conversations and providing information, start to create an expectation of content rather than just form. Gradually promote a spirit of debate among team members too, or at least help people understand that it is acceptable to bring differing viewpoints to you, regardless of someone's ranking and power in the group.

Such a process will be difficult and will only develop slowly among the Chinese managers, as it runs counter to their culture. But it must be done; otherwise, your meetings will never move beyond being superficial, perfunctory rituals to report facts and data, devoid of group discussion and problem solving.

Stage 2: Work with Your Senior Team to Determine the Appropriate Vision and Strategy

The second stage is to get the managers who lead your team(s) to help you build a shared vision and strategy for the way forward. Common ground must be found. There are different ways to create agreement. The following approaches work both outside and within China.

Help Your Management Team and Key Employees Understand the Business

Local managers who have never worked in a multinational company often do not have a clear understanding of how Western businesses operate. For instance, they do not realize the importance of profit, integrity, or protecting the company's proprietary information. Often, they also have yet to learn other aspects of business, such as what is important for customers, growth drivers, etc. Have your senior expatriate managers provide structured training on business fundamentals for your China team. An alternative is to conduct this training yourself, which would have two advantages:

- It builds your credibility. Sharing your experience and knowledge demonstrates your management and leadership credentials to your team. Chinese employees expect leaders to have strong industry and functional expertise to qualify them as a leader.
- It allows you to demonstrate your passion to the team.

An effective technique for helping your key reports become more business savvy is to have them experience a business simulation, such as DDI's *Making Sense of Business: A Simulation*® or *Strategic Leadership Experience*®. You then can augment the insights they gain by pointing out similarities within their own areas of responsibility. Often, people are more open to discussing situations in a simulation's hypothetical company than they are to discussing real-life issues in their own organization. The simulation provides neutral ground to delve into these areas.

Expand Your Direct Reports' Thinking

Organizations tend to develop a functional blindness to their own problems and opportunities, which often remain unnoticed—or at least not acted upon—until something catastrophic happens. You can flesh out problems and opportunities by encouraging your reports to view their situation differently. For example, you can ask them to identify the most critical beliefs that have shaped the company's view of itself in the past five years, and then ask them to nominate the beliefs most needed for the journey forward. Your team can work in small groups to come up with lists of old and new beliefs and then hone them down in a larger group meeting. During the discussion you might float some trial balloons about both the old and new beliefs to gain more insights into their thinking.

New Paradigms for Your Management Team

The following is an example of old and new beliefs worked out by a team of managers in a manufacturing operation in China during several discussions set up by their country manager.

Old Beliefs

> **Work toward maximum output**—Managers believe that more business and more production mean more profits.

> **Stress unit success over organizational success**—This is a company very much divided by units (silos).

> **Allocate resources by functions**—Each unit seeks resources and makes plans based on its own needs.

> **Stress working hard**—Managers believe that hard work will give them the edge on competitors.

> **Focus on task and technical solutions**—Managers devise technical solutions to problems. Little thought is given to the effects on employees or customers.

New Beliefs

> **Know customer needs and market demand**—Grow those areas that can provide an edge to customers and do so profitably.

> **Focus on overall business performance**—Hone in on overall business performance with short- and long-term goals, rather than the success of individual units.

> **Base resource allocation on strategic focus**—Allocate resources based on the company's overall strategic focus.

> **Be proactive on problems**—Build infrastructure and management control systems to prevent problems, rather than waiting for problems to develop and then attempting to solve them.

> **Develop a more people-oriented focus**—Challenge managers to provide a better work environment.

Another good idea is to invite industry experts to talk with your senior team about trends and best practices.

Show the Courage to Have Convictions

The process of setting a direction is not just analytical; it takes courage to decide where you want the organization to go and commitment to go there. Heroic leadership is a strongly admired traditional Chinese value. In the context of China's current economic boom, leaders who exude courage can accomplish a great deal. Chinese employees will be highly motivated if they know their leader has set a bold, audacious goal with a specific timeline.

Your Chinese employees, of course, see you as representing the interests of the Western partners, even if the organization is not a joint venture, because you come from outside. They want to know what difference you plan to make for yourself, the team, and the company. And they want to know that achieving your goals will benefit them as well as China's economic and social development in general.

Your conviction to achieve your business goal won't be real to your Chinese employees unless they perceive that you are driving consistently toward it. In day-to-day decisions, they expect you to take a stand on big and small issues and to handle controversial matters. Taking a stand and making decisions represent your first accreditation stamp in being seen as qualified in a "leadership" position. If your Chinese employees believe you are not willing to stand firm, they won't follow you. Ambiguity about direction is not seen as a good leadership trait in Chinese culture.

Stage 3: Communicate Your Plans and Get Buy-In

Three tactics are useful for getting your Chinese managers to buy into your strategy and goals:
- Send key local managers overseas on a benchmarking trip, perhaps to corporate headquarters or to another overseas operation.
- Explain what the new direction means for each level of employee.
- Align the company's vision with Chinese nationalistic sentiment.

Send a Team to Benchmark an Overseas Operation

Often your team members will have difficulty visualizing the new direction you are proposing. You can remedy this by allowing key people to travel overseas to observe how the same issues (e.g., higher quality standards, more control over vendor quality) have been successfully handled elsewhere. Overseas benchmarking trips open eyes and soften resistance to change. Exposing your key Chinese staff to new ways of doing things will teach them to become more visionary themselves. After the benchmarking trips, they will develop their own ideas and become your change agents.

What needs to be considered when planning such a benchmarking trip? Who will likely absorb the most and come back and act as change agents, helping to drive the new direction? High-potential team members are important, as are those who are skilled at influencing others. The staff you choose for the trip also should be passionate in their interest in the team and the company, quick at learning and spotting new opportunities, and seen by local employees as leaders in terms of the respect they command and their ability to shape opinion. Because it is unusual for a single person to have all these qualities, it is best to assemble and send a select team.

"Lean" Manufacturing Is Hard to Understand Until It Is Seen in Action

Many manufacturing operations in China can benefit from the introduction of lean manufacturing, with its continual emphasis on eliminating waste, improving product quality, and reducing cost and production time.

Expatriate managers who are trying to introduce empowered lean manufacturing teams in their Chinese operations have found it extremely beneficial to send key influential employees, supervisors, and middle managers to other factories where such teams operate effectively. Doing so lets them observe how things are done and talk with the people involved. The same is true when a new technology or work standard is being introduced.

If set up correctly, these overseas trips will help the individuals return as local experts and leaders of the change that is to be introduced to the China operation.

Explain What the New Direction Means for Each Level of Employee

When a new direction is introduced, your employees will, of course, want to know what will be required of them as well as what's in it for them. You will need answers to the following questions:

- What training and development opportunities will be provided to employees? How will the company's career-advancement opportunities change? Will the change affect the organization's plans for localization of management?
- Will localization be accelerated or slowed?
- Will compensation change? Will there be stock options or other incentives (e.g., housing, mortgage loans, overseas scholarships for employees, overseas assignments) to encourage employees to accept the changes being made?

Expatriate managers need to be visionaries who are able to convey an image of the company's future state to their team. Expatriate managers who are (or give the appearance of being) focused only on the short term—or who are on a short-term assignment—will not inspire confidence. Many Chinese in multinationals have had bad experiences with revolving-door expatriate managers.

Align the Company's Vision with Chinese Nationalistic Sentiment

As has been mentioned already, the Chinese are becoming more nationalistic. China's government and the Chinese media are fostering this feeling. Foreign investment is welcome, but that sentiment can quickly change if it seems that China's interests are being harmed or ignored. Here are some questions you will need to answer:

- What is the expansion/growth plan for the company in China? What will be the investment, sales, and revenue growth, and the number of employees in three to five years?

- What role will the China operation play in the company's overall global strategy? For example, will China be the regional head office in Asia? Will China be the biggest market for the company?

- What technology will be transferred to China? Will there be research and development capability in China? How soon and how big will it be?

- How will the company's growth affect the growth of the specific industry in China?

- What will be the company's contribution to the local community and its institutions? Will there be donations or partnership programs with universities, research centers, education donation programs for the inner rural cities, and local social welfare organizations?

In summary, your Chinese employees will want to know the short-term benefits (what they will get) and the longer-term prospects for the company, particularly relative to what other companies will be doing and offering, as well as the broader context of how your operation will serve China's interests. Chinese employees tend to entrust their hopes to the company, and they want to be on a winning team. "You need a leadership team that is able to articulate a vision that makes employees willing to go forward," remarked P.C. Loh, vice president and executive managing director of Spansion China, which was rated as the Best Employer in Asia in 2007.[1]

Remember too that in a society that is now very Internet savvy, the local employees will be able to quickly see what analysts abroad and the head office are saying about the company and its China operations. Make sure the message from the China operation is in accord with what is communicated elsewhere.

Says one expatriate manager, "In China, you need to be a great communicator, articulating both the short- and long-term vision to your employees, all the time. You need to keep repeating your vision to them." This helps to remind them of the vision and reassures your team. But it's also essential because with China's buoyant labor market, your team is likely to be growing or turning over—or both—to some degree.

Getting the Message Right

Getting the public relations right is essential in China. Here are two examples of how companies have communicated the alignment of corporate interests with China's interests.

IBM Launches a Major Services Initiative in China

IBM Chairman, President, and CEO Samuel J. Palmisano, speaking in China on November 13, 2006:

> "IBM has a long history of collaborating with our Chinese clients and with the government of China in support of the country's rapid economic development. . . . This services initiative will strengthen our role as China's innovation partner based on our portfolio of the world's best technology combined with our business management and services skills. The announcements we are making today strengthen our ability to help develop future services skills in China while providing solutions now to meet the needs of the evolving Chinese economy." [2]

Royal Philips Electronics in China

Gerard Kleisterlee, president and CEO of Royal Philips Electronics, speaking at the European Foundation for Quality Management Forum, Cardiff, U.K., on October 4, 2005:

> "We are proud to be the largest multinational company in China as measured by overall sales, as well as being one of the largest investors in China. We formed our first China joint venture in 1985—currently, we have around 35 legal entities in the country between joint-ventures and subsidiaries. Today, we employ around 20,000 people in China and our total business activity is around [US$]9 billion. . . . China is not only a competitor but also a rapidly growing market for products and services, a real growth engine for the world economy." [3]

Keep asking your employees if they feel that the vision—the direction—that you and the company are taking is "workable" in China. An unequivocal "yes" is good news. A muted response qualified with the need to recognize *guo qing*—that is, mainland Chinese ways—suggests that your vision is not yet fully understood and shared by your local employees. It might be time for another look at your communications plan and maybe even a reassessment and some fine-tuning of your strategy.

CHAPTER 7

Getting Your Team to Act Like a Team

Teamwork in China is a challenge. This might surprise those who think of Asian cultures as community-minded and harmonious, but in China the reality is different. Traditionally, this society was not based on a broad sense of community so much as along family and clan lines. Teamwork within families is commonplace, but teamwork among otherwise unrelated and unconnected individuals has little historical precedent. Also, given the scarce-resources mentality that has been discussed earlier in these pages, there is little natural tendency for teamwork. All this means that teamwork does not come naturally in China at either the junior or senior level.

Young people born in the 1980s and later (known as the "Post '80s," "Little Emperors," or sometimes as the "Praised Generation" because of all the positive reinforcement they received while growing up) now occupy the junior levels of most office environments in China. They tend to operate individually, working against each other to show up their colleagues. They are less willing to share knowledge, information, and useful contacts; to them, sharing such resources limits their chances for individual success and for looking good compared to their colleagues.

When local employees are organized into a team, there will be a tendency for talking, rather than listening. This talking should not be mistaken for interaction. Little cooperation will occur, and plans often will fail because team members will not be inclined to follow team rules.

Following

As an expatriate, you instantly will be seen as a leader in China, regardless of your previous experience or position in the organization. This fact has wide-reaching implications for you as a manager. It will have a direct impact on how you need to perform, because you will always be "on stage," under constant scrutiny. Your staff will be looking to follow your lead.

For most Chinese, following is a more ingrained behavior than working as part of a team. Chinese staff are good followers if they have a strong, competent leader with whom they can identify. As followers, they are reliable, discrete, and loyal; they try hard to empathize with their leader. In contrast with many employees in the West, whose loyalty is more anchored on the goal and the psychological feeling of owning the task, Chinese employees actually feel emotional ties to their leader. In China the leader must project a strong vision, have obvious expertise and thus credibility, be prepared to stand up for his or her staff, and demonstrate loyalty to them. Strong leadership is essential, but there is one significant cost: When a strong leader leaves the company, often his or her followers will do the same. This possibility needs to be accounted for and remedial strategies put in place to combat it.

How to Develop Teamwork

Stage One: Be Careful Whom You Select as Team Leaders

Obviously, selection is key—you need to choose the right people for team leadership positions, both in the eyes of senior management and the local employees. Also, when selecting team members, their ability and motivation to work in teams should be prime considerations.

Stage Two: Provide Leadership Training

Leadership training and development for existing and potential managers is critical in helping them make the transition from followers to leaders. It is important that the training not just teach theories, but provide models of good leadership—for example, showing videos of effective leaders handling difficult team situations. Many young Chinese managers have not seen models of effective individual or team leadership. Their parents—working in the bureaucratic setting of state enterprises—likely would have told them stories not of leadership, but authority.

A special training challenge occurs when a young Chinese employee is chosen to be a team leader. The young team leader must learn how to respect older team members and still be effective in his or her leadership role, because, to a large extent, the loyalty and contributions of older members will determine the team's success.

Providing leadership training is one thing, but there also must be adequate follow-up to ensure that the newly learned concepts and skills are applied on the job. To reinforce the training, you, as the expatriate manager, must follow the training precepts and demonstrate the effective behaviors in meetings with your management team. By seeing you in action modeling the leadership behaviors, your local managers will better understand what they need to do and why the new leadership behaviors are important. Following your lead, they will become progressively more effective in taking on team leadership roles.

Stage Three: Teach Cooperation Skills

When fostering teamwork in China, it is a good idea to establish ground rules. Basics that might be assumed elsewhere should not be taken for granted. An example of a "Team Contract" was featured in Chapter 5. The following norms for successful teamwork also can function like a team contract—they must be spelled out, accepted, and observed by your team.

- **Accomplish team goals first**—The team's goals and their accomplishment should take priority over any individual goals.

- **Utilize one another's skills**—The team agrees on each member's role and accountability as well as how it will use each member's skills and expertise.

- **Support one another**—No one person can achieve the team goal all alone. Team members need to see how they can support each other to accomplish the group's objective. They must learn how to solve conflicts among themselves in a constructive manner and without appealing to more senior staff for resolution.

- **Listen to others**—Openly hearing different points of view can help the team reach a better solution. Listening also involves the emotional support and empathy that team members give one another when facing difficulties.

- **Execute team agreements**—Accomplishing results depends on how well team members can execute the team's agreed-upon actions. It is imperative, then, that team members truly buy into the agreement and contribute their best skills and efforts so that the team can achieve its goals.

Teams function best when their members contribute equally and have equal footing. Younger Chinese employees might learn team skills relatively quickly; older or more-senior team members could take longer. Also, older Chinese staff might find it difficult to let younger team members play meaningful roles. Changing this deeply ingrained practice will prove very difficult, but appropriate training can help.

Recognizing and rewarding positive team behaviors will help the new behaviors take root. For example, you might give out "high-performing team" or "partnership" awards. Such awards are more symbolic and "face giving" than financial. You also can treat the team to a celebration dinner—Chinese managers like celebration dinners. You can further reinforce desired team behaviors by publicizing stories of other teams' exemplary behaviors and how successful teams have helped to achieve overall company or customer satisfaction targets.

Stage Four: Insist That Teams Develop a Charter

A team charter, driven by the leader with participation from all team members, will formalize the team's:

- Purpose.
- Accountabilities.
- Goals.
- Ground rules.

Spending time up front discussing the charter will pay off later by reducing miscommunication and wasted time in meetings.

Possible Elements of a Team Charter

> What is the team's purpose?

> What is the team's final product?

> How will the team measure its success?

> Are there any deadlines, and if so, what are they?

> What types of decisions can team members make independently?

> What are the ground rules for interacting and collaborating with each other (e.g., following through on promises)?

> Are there any budgetary or other resource limitations?

> Are there restrictions on the team's final recommendations or decisions? If so, what are they?

> What types of training or support will be provided to team members?

> How often will the team meet, and how will meetings be run? What preparations will be expected for team meetings (e.g., agenda, pre-reading materials, etc.)?

Stage Five: Teach Leaders to Collaborate Across Teams

A challenge in China is getting teams to work collectively. Team leaders must be encouraged to collaborate among themselves. And again, this must be done in the context of the strong leader–follower culture. Members of different teams will cooperate if they see their respective team leaders cooperating. This can be accomplished by tying rewards and credit to leaders' inter-team collaboration. Credit given by a top leader is particularly valued in a face-oriented culture. And so senior managers—expatriate or otherwise—have an important role here. As senior managers, they need to consciously manage the sharing of credit among teams.

There is a subtle difference between credit and recognition. Recognition is similar to praise, which is good but not strong enough in the Chinese context. In Chinese thinking, *credit* refers to the leader's recognition of the team's efforts *and* results. Chinese want to know how they contributed to the leader's success rather than simply being thanked for their efforts. The leader needs to share the credit—across teams and managers.

Managing Credit Among Team Leaders

Kent, the CEO of a transportation company in Southern China, knows that three core teams—sales, logistics, and public and government relations—must collaborate if the company is to meet its targets.

On the surface it appears that the sales department should get the most credit for the sales revenue. But Kent knows that without the logistics and public relations departments, the sales would not have been realized. The PR department plays an important role in maintaining good relations with the local government, which regulates the transportation industry. In addition, a great deal of business comes from the government sector. The logistics department is responsible for daily operations. So these two supporting functions make a significant, although less visible, contribution.

Kent knows that he must be careful to balance the credit among these three teams, each of which is headed by an experienced local manager. So, in meetings Kent lavishes credit on the logistics and PR groups, explaining how their hard work and contributions are essential to the company. As a result, these two supporting departments feel that in the eyes of their leader, they are not inferior to the sales department; in fact, they are respected as catalysts that drive the business. Kent knows this balancing act is important in China to keep these teams working hard and collaborating.

Take Action with Underachievers

Not all team members will be able to progress at the same speed. In fact, some may show little progress at all, so there is one aspect of Chinese leadership style that expatriate managers should not adapt: tolerating underachievers.

No matter how poor a team member's performance, Chinese managers typically prefer not to drop anyone from their teams—particularly if the underachiever has proven to be a loyal follower. Such tolerance for poor performance is not appropriate for Western companies seeking to develop performance-driven operations in China.

Poor performers need to be handled delicately in China, but they should not be tolerated. Strategies to turn around their behavior or, if necessary, to arrange for their exit need to be developed. Chapter 10 delves more deeply into dealing with poor performers.

CHAPTER 8

Training Your Employees

Training your staff is important everywhere; in China you cannot afford not to train your Chinese employees. Training serves several key purposes in China:

- Young employees regard the training provided as one of the key criteria for selecting and staying with an organization. Training programs help employees feel valued by their company.
- It fills skill gaps in your workforce. As discussed in previous chapters, the quality of university graduates is not as high as most organizations would desire, particularly when they reach the middle and senior levels of management. Boards of directors and CEOs readily recognize that the failure to groom adequate leadership talent can become the largest impediment to growth and success in China.
- It helps your employees understand and internalize your corporate values and your expectations of those values.

This chapter discusses training for two different groups: local managers and non-management employees.

Training Your Chinese Managers

DDI's 2005 report, *Leadership in China: Keeping Pace with a Growing Economy*, found that the most critical skills for Chinese leaders are motivating others, building trust, retaining talent, and developing and then leading high-performance teams.[1] But many managers in the study were found to be weak in these skills. Many have taken a more traditional Chinese approach, which is incompatible with today's global environment and unlikely to fit in with the corporate culture of the typical modern or Western organization.

Leadership training is essential to help your Chinese managers develop the skills they need. They must be equipped to be able to develop in their own reports a clear understanding of and confidence in the company's strategic direction, foster a highly participative environment, motivate others for change, and facilitate functional collaboration among organizational units as they work on common challenges.

Training programs are most effective if delivered when they are needed (for example, when moving from one job level to another). Like building blocks forming a structure, training programs need to complement each other, especially in concepts and terminology. The building block approach has the strength of a pyramid—building upon and reinforcing itself—allowing managers to expand on and add to their existing abilities in a logical progression. And, like a pyramid, it gives them a wide base. Plus, offering a broad slate of training demonstrates an organization's long-term commitment to employee development.

The DDI survey identified four themes for management/leadership training that are of particular value in China:[2]

- Delivering results
- Relationship building
- Coaching and development
- Managing performance

Delivering Results

Managers need training that will broaden both their business perspective and sense of ownership of the results so they can run their units as if they were their own businesses. But they do have to learn that results must be achieved by the team, not by their own work. To do this, managers must learn how to create an environment that empowers their direct reports and decentralizes the decision-making authority. This is no small feat. It requires a considerable culture change in a society of centralized authority, especially when such centralization is viewed as appropriate by most citizens.

Relationship Building

Training programs should build on Chinese notions of *guanxi* while helping managers extend beyond their innate relationship-building skills to foster a trusting environment—one in which there is ample collaboration even when there are differences. Managers also should learn how to influence others (such as their boss, peers, and reports) and become agents for change.

Coaching and Development

Managers need training that bolsters their skills in coaching, providing support, and creating development opportunities for their direct reports. The training also should build their communication skills as well as their ability to strengthen employees' commitment to the company's vision and values.

Managing Performance

Training programs should address managers' ability to keep their teams performing at consistently high levels and on track with the organization's strategy and goals. In a competitive environment there is no room for misdirected effort and poor performance. Managers must be able to review progress toward agreed-upon expectations, follow up and support improvement, and confront poor performance or inappropriate work habits. Proactively, managers also need to know how to create an environment for encouraging bottom-up innovation, ensuring that good ideas can be channeled upward and have the support needed to be executed.

A Structured Training Curriculum at XYZ Pharmaceuticals

Henry heads up the human resources group for XYZ Pharmaceuticals, which is headquartered in Germany. He is responsible for providing HR support to the leadership team in China, where there is a manufacturing site and a sales force. Henry makes frequent trips to the China office. One of his mandates for this year is to set up a structured training curriculum in China that will benefit both sales and manufacturing. After consulting both the expatriate and local managers and using the results of the annual 360-degree leadership survey (discussed in chapter 5), Henry proposes the following curriculum.

Target Group to Be Trained	Leadership Competency Themes			
	Delivering Results	Relationship Building	Coaching & Development	Managing Performance
First-Time Managers	• Understanding how the company makes profit • Interviewing skills for selecting the right talent • Delegating for results	• Getting started as a new leader • Essentials of leadership • Building an environment of trust • Influential leadership	• Communicating company vision and values • Coaching for success • Coaching for improvement • Leading change	• Setting performance expectations • Reviewing performance progress • Managing performance problems
Managers of Managers	• Rapid decision making • Motivating others	• Building partnerships • Retaining talent • Social intelligence	• Leading high-performance teams • Developing others	• Executing business strategy • Encouraging innovation

The proposal was approved with the full support of the leadership team in China. The China GM knows that training is not only important, but urgent.

Most of the curriculum Henry developed comprises a behavior modeling approach, because that method is well accepted by Chinese leaders. The underlying philosophy for behavior modeling is "See, try, and apply." This approach enables Chinese leaders to see what is required, try the skills in a safe learning environment, and then apply them back on the job. Also, it is a refreshing approach when compared to the traditional learning method of listening to a lecture on theory followed by taking a test.

One Participant's Reaction to the Training at XYZ Pharmaceuticals

Jifu Zou joined XYZ Pharmaceuticals four months ago. This is his second job since leaving a position in a government-run hospital where he'd worked since graduation. He made the move after the promise of better pay. Jifu's first job after leaving the hospital was as a sales representative for a state-owned pharmaceutical company. He stayed with the company for less than two years before joining XYZ Pharmaceuticals. In his new job Jifu leads a small team of young sales representatives who have recently graduated from school.

He attends "Coaching for Success," the first course in the learning road map. When he arrives for training, Jifu notices that the classroom setup is different from any training he has ever attended. Participants are required to sit in table teams. In training sessions while in his previous jobs, he remembers participants sitting next to each other, listening and diligently taking notes as the teacher spoke. Communication was definitely one-way.

The facilitator warmly welcomes Jifu, who is ready for a new learning experience. The program starts promptly at 8:45 a.m. with about 20 participants. Jifu takes the following notes on what he finds useful as well as on the program's flow:

What Happened	My Reaction
Facilitator prompts discussion about the coaching role.	I do not volunteer for this round of discussion, but I take notes on others' views.
Participants are asked to discuss high performance and identify characteristics of a high-performing person or group.	I participate in the small group discussion.
In a small team, participants are asked to define coaching and its goals. The class watches a video on how to create an environment in which people seek coaching and strive to be high performers.	The group asks me to report its ideas to the class, and I do so.
Facilitator reviews the interaction process relative to conducting coaching discussions.	I take more notes.

What Happened (cont'd)	My Reaction (cont'd)
Participants discuss two positive models from the video that highlight coaching steps and stress striking a balance between seeking and telling.	I am impressed that a number of "face-giving" techniques are used in the video. The manager in the video asks good questions—something I don't usually feel comfortable doing myself.
In trials, participants practice using the skills—one assumes a role as the manager, one as the employee, and one as the observer. Time is allotted for preparation, and at the end of the skill practice, the observer and employee give detailed feedback using the guided questions from the role-play sheet. All participants get to assume all three roles (manager, employee, and observer) in the training session.	When it was my turn to act as the manager, I was nervous for the first few minutes, particularly as I had to role-play in front of colleagues. I felt relieved at the end of the discussion, and I found the feedback from my colleagues useful. It gave me insights on what I might do differently in future coaching situations.

Jifu finds this training a rewarding experience and feels excited about using the new skills back at his workplace. He looks forward to the next training course, which will be in one week.

Training Your Non-Management Chinese Employees

Non-management Chinese employees (e.g., salespeople, professionals, scientists) also need training beyond the technical expertise of their function. In addition to the job skills training, most benefit from the following:

- Corporate citizenship training
- Business literacy training
- Non-technical skills training
- Career self-management

Corporate Citizenship Training

To get employees to understand and live the corporate values, it is important to foster greater identification with the organization. Promoting a sense of interdependence and pride in one's company is synchronous with the Chinese emphasis on family and group. Greater pride in the company will help with employee retention, something borne out in surveys of the Best Employers in China by Hewitt Associates.[3]

Corporate Citizenship Training at XYZ Pharmaceuticals

Henry's job involves more than simply setting up the management development curriculum. He also supports the leadership team, providing structured training for employees. One of his objectives for employee training is to redesign the company orientation program. Instead of a half-day event dominated by one-way communication (i.e., a lecture) and benefits briefings, Henry worked with the local HR team to design a three-day acculturation training program, detailed below.

The program's intent was to get employees to understand the company's culture, motivate them, and reinforce their decision to join the organization. Henry worked with the local HR team to design the content. Although the local team was not experienced in program design, it learned quickly through Henry's efforts. He also trained three local HR personnel—each of whom will partner with a line manager—to deliver the program.

	Day 1	Day 2	Day 3
Morning session	• Company vision, global business outlook	• China business outlook and plan for next five years	• Developing your career
Afternoon session	• Living the company's values • Ethics overview	• Introduction to performance management	• Next 90 days: How to make a fast start
Evening session	• Meeting with star performers	• Dialog with China CEO or COO	

As always, corporate training efforts need to be mindful of the Chinese culture, as values can be interpreted differently. Consider the examples in Table 8.1.

TABLE 8.1: Examples of Contrasting Cultural Values

Values	Western Concept	Chinese Concept
Integrity	• The concept of legality can be somewhat subjective (e.g., driving over the speed limit is often tolerated). • Honesty. • Deliver what is promised. • Bribery is defined as any non-business act, gift, or favor given for the purpose of advancing personal interests or business deals.	• Legality is much more subjective. • Maintaining relationships is part of one's integrity. • Details are often left to interpretation. • Gifts/Entertainment/Special privileges do not constitute bribery.
Initiative	• Taking action without being asked. • Putting in the extra effort to meet or exceed customer expectations.	• Actions must fall within "defined" rules and boundaries. • Taking initiative is doing the other person a favor or building a personal relationship.

You cannot assume that your China employees will understand or agree with the message you are trying to instill. "It's not about translating into Chinese and having a poster on the wall . . ." says Nora Hughes, organizational development manager for Intel group. "They need for these things to make sense in their own culture."[4] Training programs can help provide a vivid demonstration of the new expected culture and standards. Seeing how those standards play out in positive video models supported by discussions can accelerate understanding of the standards and desired workplace behaviors.

One fundamental development need for Chinese leaders is training in integrity and business ethics. Because many Western companies have higher business ethical standards than their Chinese counterparts, it is imperative to clearly define expectations regarding how a company's values should drive its employees' decisions and actions. However, past practices show that a directive lecture does not automatically lead to mutual understanding. A two-way dialog via the training process can not only help people understand the new required standards, but also afford you an opportunity to make acceptable adaptations to your corporate values. For example, foreign companies might relax the definition of bribery to exclude gift presentations if management is informed of them in advance. Some companies feel this is a reasonable concession; in Chinese culture, for instance, refusal of a gift is likely to lead to the giver losing face.

Business Literacy Training

This category of training aims to enhance Chinese employees' understanding of business basics—how companies make money and create value for their customers. Such training would be beneficial for those employees who have strong professional skills in one discipline but who need to broaden their expertise to see the connections with other disciplines.

The most common training teaches employees skills such as how to read profit-and-loss statements and understand the internal rate of return. However, the best companies focus their training on the basics of how organizations operate and how decisions are made. Using business simulations is an effective—and, in China, very popular—way of providing such training. Table 8.2 sets out a basic business skills program for two levels of employees.

TABLE 8.2: Example of a Business Literacy Program

Level	Business Literacy Training
Professional Staff	• How companies make money. • How we create value for our customers.
Managers	• Understanding business decisions. • Investing and leveraging company assets.

Non-Technical Skills Training

Typically, even the best professional staff in China lack certain behavioral skills, no matter how strong their professional qualifications. Communication, collaboration, working in teams, creative thinking, problem solving, and career self-management are common among the skills that might need to be acquired or improved upon.

- **Communication, collaboration, and teamwork skills**—These include active listening and interpersonal skills. Topics covered would include how to collaborate with other team members, how to share best practices across the organization, and how to network more effectively with customers and key members of the organization. Team skills training in China needs to embrace both awareness and skill development. The need for team collaboration skills training was discussed in Chapter 7.

- **Creative-thinking and problem-solving skills**—This training is crucial. Chinese employees expect their leaders to take responsibility for developing solutions. They might even view taking the initiative to develop solutions themselves as potentially undermining their traditional Chinese leaders.

However, today's business environment requires employees to solve problems for themselves, especially regarding improving or streamlining their work processes. Doing so requires them to think creatively, ask questions, seek clarification when they don't understand, and suggest improvements. Employees need to learn how to go beyond superficial solutions—a problem needs to be attacked, not papered over.

In China, training for creative thinking and problem solving should include:

- Recognizing and defining problems, implementing solutions, taking action, and tracking and evaluating results.
- Influencing others, resolving conflict, and knowing when and how to escalate problems to senior levels.
- Thinking laterally, challenging assumptions, and generating new options.

The more contact your Chinese professionals have with Westerners and those from a Western education environment, the more they will recognize that they have these development needs and others related to Western business norms. And they will be eager to learn new skills that will enable them to proactively improve their performance and marketability. This will be one of the most difficult areas to develop because it involves undoing years of rote learning and living in a culture that traditionally demands unquestioned following.

Non-Technical Behavioral Skills Training at XYZ Pharmaceuticals

Henry knows that behavioral competency training will be difficult. The company has several locations in China, and the training materials must be in Chinese. Fortunately, he was able to find an international vendor that could provide its materials translated and adapted to the Chinese culture. Henry works quickly with the company's leadership team to identify six line managers to be trained as in-house facilitators. This training is usually held on Friday afternoons, and each course is followed by an employee get-together where several more line managers join them. All learners are required to complete a "learning road map" as agreed with their boss and to take two or three competency clusters selected through consultation with their boss.

Competency Clusters	Courses (3–4 hours each)
1. Communication	• Communicating with others
	• Supporting others
2. Communication and Teamwork	• Working in teams
	• Reaching agreement in teams
	• Participating effectively in meetings
	• Leading effective meetings
	• Rescuing difficult meetings
3. Solving Problems in Teams and Continuous Improvement	• Creative thinking tools and techniques
	• Identifying improvement opportunities
	• Taking actions for improvement
	• Sustaining improvement
	• Resolving conflict
4. Career Self-Management	• Empowering yourself
	• Giving and receiving feedback
	• Growing your skills

Career Self-Management

This training develops skills that will enable employees to increase the value they can add to their current and future jobs. Without this training, the gap between their ambitions and their career progress can make them vulnerable to poachers.

Career self-management training also includes skills for self-improvement, such as giving and receiving feedback and how to deal positively with a career setback. Teaching Chinese employees career management skills can make them more open to accepting tough performance feedback and more resilient to career ups and downs.

Options for Delivering Training

Options for delivery vary according to the training's purpose. If it is geared to skill development, requiring learners' active participation, then plenty of practice in small groups is needed. A common development option would be to engage external experts or specially trained internal facilitators to conduct the learning sessions. If the content is mostly knowledge-based information, then an organization's intranet might be the most cost-effective mode of delivery. Combinations of classroom training and self-learning via the intranet can be useful as well. For example, some companies provide online orientation programs to cover the company's history, products, and market information in combination with live dialog sessions with senior executives that focus on business strategy, the China business outlook, company values, and career development within the organization.

Business cases (either general business or company-specific cases) are another mode of training that works well in China. Cases describing successful Chinese companies or Western case studies translated into Chinese are available on the market. Participants familiarize themselves with the case first, and then discuss it and develop solutions to problems during training sessions. Such discussions require a skilled facilitator.

Computer-based business simulations that allow groups to compete with one another also work well in China, as young Chinese employees tend to enjoy competitive situations. Some companies create teams of participants from different locations and business units and then get them to compete against other teams in simulations that might last for two days. In addition to developing business and judgment skills, this builds team skills and gets participants accustomed to cooperating with people outside their own business unit or silo.

Exercises that involve physical activity and outdoor training, such as rock climbing, also work well in China. They are good for team building, either for existing teams or cross-functional teams. Getting teams involved in outdoor activities creates energy, challenge, and fun, but does not substitute for specific skills training.

Many training options are available in China; the trick is how to make the training content and methodology fit the Chinese culture. DDI is one major training company to offer programs especially adapted for the Chinese culture. University providers of learning programs are common in China as well. Their effectiveness depends on the quality of their faculties, how much they concentrate on actual skill development, and the degree to which they are willing to adjust their course curricula to specific company needs.

Some foreign companies have developed their own corporate "universities," giving them the capacity to provide a broad range of training and learning activities for their employees. A world-class corporate university in China can help enormously with employer branding.

Teams Training at XYZ Pharmaceuticals

Fucan Zhang was recruited fresh from university to a research unit at XYZ Pharmaceuticals. The first training course on his learning road map was "Working in a Team." Before attending the training program, Fucan felt uncertain about its value. He believed that being a successful researcher meant simply excelling at research and product development. He did not see how teamwork fit into his job.

The training started with a simulation. Fucan was among 20 participants organized into four teams, and each team needed to complete a task according to quality and timeline requirements. Given the time pressure and the pressure from the other teams, Fucan decided that it would be best to work with his team. It would have been a loss of face if his team failed, particularly if it looked as if he hadn't given his best effort or contributed.

After the simulation the facilitator led a discussion on team success factors, such as purpose, communication, process, continuous improvement, and trust. Then the teams were asked to participate in a second round of the simulation, but this time with more focus on cost reduction, quality improvement, and timeliness.

Fucan's team exceeded the "stretch goals," and he felt pleased. By the end of the training, he was thinking about how he could begin collaborating with others so that he might reach his ultimate goal of coming up with a breakthrough new product.

Training tends to be under-provided in China, particularly in many Chinese companies that prefer to see investment in tangibles such as plant and equipment rather than intangibles such as staff development. But training is essential everywhere, and nowhere is that truer than in China, where new skills need to be instilled and old ways and thinking must be undone. Rarely will employees arrive in a new company "ready-made." Organizations either must have a comprehensive, structured internal training program for their employees, or they must outsource such programs to outside professionals who are able to modify their offerings for the Chinese environment. Training helps with recruitment, retention, and, of course, performance. Economizing on this expense—and it can be a considerable expense in China—will prove a false economy. This chapter has focused on training options you will need to consider in China. The next chapter looks at a complementary consideration: effectively coaching your China reports.

第9章

CHAPTER 9

Coaching Your Team

Although people have different abilities and educational levels, everyone has the capacity to grow. What usually holds them back is not knowing what direction that growth should take—that is, what skills they should acquire or hone. While there are many formal types of training that can aid their development, the main means of skills growth is the coaching and teaching provided by an employee's immediate supervisor.

Coaching is an essential skill for managers everywhere, especially in China, where you can expect to be more of a coach than you have ever been before. Your staff will look to you for coaching, and because of your efforts, they will be more inclined to stay with your company. But as DDI's competency surveys have found, coaching is not a strength of many expatriate managers. This skill gap is complicated by the distinct characteristics and development needs of the different age groups of the local employees. So, the expatriate's coaching focus is split between younger and older Chinese managers; different coaching techniques are needed for each group.

Coaching a team in China is further complicated by the importance placed on face and the desire to avoid open confrontations and even direct speech. These cultural factors cannot be avoided; you have no choice but to accommodate and work with them. In China, if you make coaching your strength, then you will win much respect from your staff as a leader and manager.

If you don't have coaching skills when taking on an assignment in China, you are strongly advised to get some training.

Coaching Younger Chinese Managers

China's rapid economic growth and the relative dearth of managerial talent mean that local managers in China—particularly in Western companies—tend to be far younger than their professional equivalents in more mature economies. They tend to be hired and promoted because of their technical skills, rather than any leadership skills. Organizations also promote many simply to keep them. This means that many expatriate managers in multinational companies typically lead teams of young managers who are in their late twenties or early thirties.

DDI's 2005 report, *Leadership in China: Keeping Pace with a Growing Economy,* found that relatively few young leaders were rated as having strengths in the most important skill areas required of good leaders, and more than half of the Chinese leaders of all ages surveyed (i.e., 55 percent) were inadequately prepared for their role in the new economy.[1]

If not coached and developed, young Chinese managers tend to acquire bad management habits. More common examples include:

- **Excessive reliance on the use of power derived from their rank**— Young managers often have a credibility problem. Their direct reports see them as only marginally more capable than they are. Similarly, young managers know there is only a small gap in experience or skills between themselves and their team members. In response, many young managers rely on the sheer power of their position, issuing commands and becoming dictatorial, which only leads to further resentment in their ranks.

- **Poor delegation skills**—Many young managers experience difficulties in making the transition to getting work done through others by delegating. They are young—as managers and as people—and they often become overwhelmed in their new positions. Most likely, these young managers were promoted as a result of their strong ambition to succeed and their individual performance. Instead of driving results through others, they often try to cover all the jobs on their team. They might be aware that this is a problem, but aren't sure what to do about it. Some develop reputations for being difficult to work for, and their team members find it easier to resign rather than to stay.

- **Old characteristics are no longer strengths**—After promotion, the raw ambition that once was a strength can become a weakness. Many young managers are expected to assume a coaching role; instead, they often tend to undercut those they see as potential competitors, mistrust high-performing direct reports, and micromanage people.

A Premature Promotion

Six months ago, Rong Zhao was promoted to manager of the customer service department and now leads a team of eight customer account representatives. Rong's boss did not want to lose him and had worked with the HR department to fast-track the promotion.

But Rong has not made a good transition to his new leadership role. For example, when Jenny, the senior customer relations rep, asked for his help, Rong, not wanting to be distracted from his work, became frustrated. He told her, "Why don't you use your common sense first? You guys can't just rely on me."

In Jenny's eyes Rong is no leader; he is just a little more experienced than she is. Jenny also suspects that he is trying to keep her away from the key accounts.

Rong believes it is important for him to personally handle the big accounts. And yet, Jenny is one of the team's high-potential members. She graduated from a top Shanghai university, and her English is excellent. Privately, Rong feels that if Jenny has too much exposure to the key customers, she will become too "powerful."

He also feels that Jenny is making some mistakes in how she is handling a key customer, but he is avoiding giving her the necessary feedback. That might be too confrontational, and besides, letting her look bad every so often will strengthen his position.

Coaching Older Chinese Managers

The development needs of older managers are different from those of younger leaders. Many of them lack both management and leadership skills, and because many have prior experience with state enterprises, they often lack exposure to Western management practices. Many expend great effort to compensate for their knowledge gaps by improving and updating their skills—perhaps taking external courses during the evenings and weekends. But still, many struggle with weaker basic skills as a result of education gaps induced by the Cultural Revolution.

Managers in more established joint venture companies tend to be older. Many have reached their positions based on their seniority or their loyalty to more senior managers. Competence might well have been a lesser criterion, if one at all. Many accepted their promotion reluctantly, as they wanted to avoid the responsibility of having to deal with people issues. Such older managers place far greater importance on workplace harmony than do younger workers. They rely on their network of contacts or generally strong interpersonal skills to get work done in what remains, after all, a relationship-oriented society. They usually maintain good internal and external networks with their peers.

They also tend to be extremely dedicated to the organization and their leaders. Having said all this, some older managers do resist change, which, after all, means risk.

Conventional Coaching Techniques for Expatriate Managers

Both younger and older Chinese managers will be uncomfortable dealing with poor performers on their teams. Maintaining face and harmony is always the preferred option, even if this is not always the reality in practice. When a team is hobbled by a poor performer, the best option is for that person to leave of his or her own accord. Cultural constraints limit many managers' ability to give adequate performance feedback and conduct performance reviews. So, a more usual strategy in China is to keep the under-performing employee in place, hoping that he or she will cause little damage, and to find a new person to perform the required role at the same or a higher organizational level. Such an arrangement hardly qualifies as sound management, but it does maintain harmony. Coaching and providing feedback are difficult tasks in China, largely because Chinese are extremely sensitive to face.

The managers who report to you will need a lot of help in dealing with performance and other common leadership issues. Here are seven basic coaching truths that can work anywhere, but that need to be applied with greater care in China:
1. You have to want to help.
2. Focus on intrinsic needs: pride and security.
3. Maintain or enhance self-esteem.
4. Listen and respond with empathy.
5. Seek ideas for solving problems.
6. Provide timely, complete behavioral feedback.
7. Create accountability for behavioral change.

1. You Have to Want to Help

Coaching means helping team members do their best. Your local managers or employees need to strongly feel your willingness to invest personally in their development. Young Chinese particularly will be sensitive as to whether they have your support. Keep reminding people that you want them to succeed and that you have set high performance standards for them, which will both encourage their development and challenge them.

Give feedback aimed at helping the recipient, rather than to just get something off your chest. Cultivate an environment that encourages your staff and managers to ask for help when they need it.

2. Focus on Intrinsic Needs: Pride and Security

One way to reduce older managers' resistance to change is to arouse their pride in what they bring to the team. For instance, the older generation is geared more to "collectivism." If they see that change will bring benefits to the group, they will be more prepared to take risks and accept it.

You can help reduce anxiety by communicating your willingness to support your team through the change process. Such reassurance is more necessary in China than in the West. Both younger and older local employees need to be reassured that if things go wrong, they will not be made scapegoats.

3. Maintain or Enhance Self-Esteem

When coaching or problem solving, be very careful to maintain or enhance the other person's self-esteem. It is very important to make people feel that you have confidence in their ability to solve a problem or handle a situation. You can do this by frequently commenting on projects an individual has handled well in the past or by citing the contributions he or she has made. This is what is meant by maintaining or enhancing self-esteem.

A word of caution: Although you might have confidence in your direct reports' ability, they might not. Showing and reinforcing your confidence in them is important, but it is also critical to always make an appropriate offer of support.

4. Listen and Respond with Empathy

People want to feel that they're being understood, both in terms of what they say and what they feel. Listening to them and then responding to their feelings encourages them to share more with you. There will be some irrelevant information that you have to deal with, but be patient; refrain from redirecting the conversation too quickly. Irrelevant information often comes from a sense of insecurity. Your managers will try as much as they can to protect themselves by passing on as much information as possible rather than trying to solve the problem directly.

Listening and responding with empathy is as important in China as anywhere.

5. Seek Ideas for Solving Problems

Most Chinese managers know the solutions to many of their own problems; they just need the confidence to take responsibility for them. Asking for your direct reports' help in coming up with alternative solutions and then weighing those alternatives will lead to superior solutions and help build their problem-solving skills. Be careful to avoid giving the impression that you are trying to understand the problem simply because you want to find whomever is responsible. If people think you are looking for someone to blame, they will be more inclined to cover up problems they encounter.

6. Provide Timely, Complete Behavioral Feedback

Try the following feedback fundamentals for a more positive result:
- State the purpose of your coaching and feedback so that the recipient understands your intentions. This is very important in China where cultural miscues can lead to unnecessary misunderstandings.
- Stick to the facts and avoid emotive words. People will respond defensively if you refer to them as "difficult," "rude," or "arrogant."
- Be specific rather than general. Talk about behavior rather than personality. People can change their behaviors, but not their personalities.
- Give feedback at the earliest opportunity.
- Provide coaching to prevent a problem. This is more effective—and easier—than coaching to correct performance.
- Refer to the effects of the behavior on other people. People are more willing to change when they learn how their actions or inactions are affecting others.
- Check for understanding. Feedback is not effective unless it is heard and understood.

7. Create Accountability for Behavioral Change

When coaching your managers, it is important for them to understand that it is their responsibility to make the transition to becoming a better manager and leader. The most direct way to do this is to hold your frontline managers accountable for the quality of their leadership as well as their technical output.

The quality of your managers' leadership can be evaluated by the quality of their selection decisions, the percentage of time they spend coaching their individual reports, the percentage of their staff who meet performance targets, their team's retention rate—especially for critical talent—and the number of people under them who are deemed ready for promotion. Coaching for results will succeed only if people are held accountable for their own behavioral changes and are rewarded for their improvement.

Modified Coaching for China

Because China is a relationship-oriented culture, conventional coaching skills need some modification. Face must be preserved as often as possible. Maintaining or enhancing self-esteem (i.e., giving face in China) is just as important for coaching poor performers as it is for coaching high potentials with excellent performance. Dressing down a poor performer in front of his or her colleagues will almost certainly have disastrous consequences and do damage that will linger, not just relative to the poor-performing employee, but also to the morale of that person's colleagues. Often, the consequences of such an interaction will not be fully apparent to the expatriate.

Usually, there will be no need to steamroll people with the facts of their poor performance. The opposite might be true. For instance, one HR professional in China is fond of recounting how, during a session on coaching skills at a global seminar, one of his multinational company's highly respected China managers explained how to coach in China. The manager told a group of 400 mostly Western company leaders that when there is a performance issue to discuss, he takes his employee for a drink and proceeds to give "light" feedback on the issue. This might not be common practice in China, but it shows the importance of being sensitive to the feedback recipients.

Here are some tips on how expatriate managers can ensure that their feedback is heard by their Chinese direct reports and acted upon:

- Clearly show your appreciation for the person's past work and contributions.
- Be prepared to listen; this is more important than questioning.
- Be patient when asking questions and tolerate pauses, if needed.
- Exercise "tough love" for Young Tigers—continually raising their performance bar and letting them know you are doing it.

Clearly show your appreciation for the person's past work and contributions—When giving corrective feedback, acknowledge what went right before you describe what went wrong. It is important to clearly show your appreciation—perhaps by commenting favorably on personal attributes, the impact of the individual's past accomplishments on the team, or the person's knowledge, local network, or desire to win and succeed. One invaluable function of older managers in China is dealing with government officials and maintaining good relations with the relevant ministry. If appropriate, this would be a good area on which to comment favorably.

Experienced Chinese managers will spend perhaps 80 percent of their corrective feedback sessions making positive statements. Of course, you don't want to overshadow the message of corrective feedback, so you must maintain delicate balance between the positive component and your corrective feedback. Avoid sugarcoating when giving positive appreciation; your appreciation should be factual, specific, and sincere.

Most likely, younger local managers will be better able to handle corrective feedback than those who are older and more concerned with face. This means that you will need to be even more sensitive when coaching older workers. They will always need to be handled carefully. If they become demotivated—perhaps because they feel they are not respected by more senior managers—older managers won't leave the company, as younger managers would do; instead, they more likely will stay and block or undermine management actions. This could cause real damage within the team.

Be prepared to listen; this is more important than questioning—Listening to someone in China is a sign of your respect; it gives face. Not only does it build trust, but it also helps expatriates better understand the local complexities.

When things are not going according to plan, it would be wise to double-check with others to see if their explanations for the setback are real and the causes unavoidable—perhaps it's because of bureaucratic holdups or some other

China-related idiosyncrasy. A staff member might not be committed to removing barriers, or perhaps there are other barriers that are difficult for an expatriate manager to understand.

Be patient when asking questions and tolerate pauses, if needed—If there is a long silence after you have asked several open-ended questions, you might feel that your coaching session has reached a dead end. Avoid the temptation to end the discussion. Instead:

- Repeat and perhaps rephrase your questions.
- Direct your questions to a more defined area, but not so much that a yes or no answer would be sufficient. You might be encouraging the staff member to reach a certain solution, but it is still up to the individual to contribute to reaching that solution. Doing so builds the person's sense of ownership.
- Consider giving the staff member an extended amount of time to think about the solution. You two can discuss it at another meeting.

Exercise "tough love" for Young Tigers—continually raising their performance bar and letting them know you are doing it—Young managers will be less perturbed by tough feedback if they understand that they still have your support. To be an effective coach to these ambitious, young Chinese managers, it is important to follow three guidelines:

1. Help them to pace themselves and direct their efforts to focus on improving just one or two critical areas. For instance, have a new Chinese manager develop an action plan to practice a certain aspect of leadership, such as:

- Defining and assigning work, and then discussing work quality with direct reports.
- Monitoring and preventing surprises (e.g., when to follow up with direct reports and how to coach them to solve problems).
- Sharing credit with others.

2. Break down goals into stages and specific evaluation targets. Instead of having a larger goal (e.g., completing a two-year project), break it down into smaller chunks that can be accomplished in less time; that way, the person gets an ongoing sense of achievement, and you have a chance to check on progress. Although they can be inspired by ambitious goals, many young managers tend to overestimate their abilities and underestimate the task at hand.

Specify the evaluation standard you will use in monitoring their efforts. Help people understand "minimal" compliance, "acceptable" compliance, and what is expected of high-potential individuals. Put your staff on notice that they can expect the performance bar to be continually raised.

3. Set aside regular coaching time to follow up on results. Also, arrange time to observe your staff in action so that when you review their progress, you can give specific feedback.

Empowering Your Local Staff

Providing high-potential candidates with needed experience must be coupled with the right delegation of authority. Some expatriate managers encounter problems of over-managing and under-leading their teams. In doing so, they take over functions that rightly belong to their reports, and they become too involved in managing more junior staff and the day-to-day operations.

Power is an important element in Chinese culture; it is important for face. If high-potential local managers are not appropriately empowered, they will be unable to advance, and inevitably they will leave the organization. Many who leave for this reason go to promising local private enterprises where they feel their progress to a prominent and empowered management role will not be impeded by the presence of expatriate managers.

Also, the expatriate manager needs to model empowerment with direct reports so they will then use the same behaviors with their own people.

Empowerment

Empowerment means giving people a sense of ownership and control over their responsibilities and a method of measuring their accomplishments. Empowerment energizes people because they feel responsible for and capable of achieving results. When things go wrong, they are motivated to remedy the situation; and when things go well, they take pride in that accomplishment.

Many expatriate and local managers do a poor job of empowering their teams. In fact, they often severely inhibit empowerment by:

> Assigning work to a person or team and then following up so closely that they feel they are not being trusted.

> Not clarifying the criteria for accomplishment, so people must keep coming to the boss to check on their progress or achievements.

> Failing to set up people for success by providing appropriate training, knowledge, or coaching when needed.

> Failing to check for understanding to be sure that assignments are clear and that people are committed to accomplishing the task at hand.

Basically, you can define the behavior required for empowerment as: "Provide support without removing responsibility for action."

Expatriate managers need to empower their Chinese reports, and those Chinese managers then need to empower their people. But remember, in the China context many local staff will only want to accept new responsibilities gradually. Too much, too soon and they might feel the pressure and want to leave. It is best to phase in empowerment, paying due regard to the cultural setting and the Chinese inclination for caution and risk avoidance.

Shaping China's Future Corporate Leaders

Developing leaders is not just about ensuring that your organization will have leaders, but that they will be *good* leaders. Here are some considerations for the talent-shaping process:

Increase people's sense of purpose—Leadership is about having a sense of purpose. It should be a tool and not an end to itself. What values do your potential leaders have and want to communicate? How will they make things better? What will be their contribution? Thinking about these sorts of issues will give your reports more direction when planning their careers.

Develop value-based leaders, not just competent leaders—In a fast-growing economy, values can be easily forgotten. It is imperative that you, as an expatriate manager in China, provide advice not just on competency issues, but also on business ethics and the company's values.

Advocate the need for strong professional talent, not just leaders—Most organizations need to develop strong professional specialists—not just generalist leaders. Because almost everyone wants to climb the organizational ladder to attain a managerial title or position, often there are too few professionals to go deep into specific disciplines. An organization must have a balanced combination of management and technical leadership.

Influence the quality of local education with corporate programs and sponsorships—Companies can influence the quality of the tertiary education in China through active involvement with universities and other tertiary education institutions around them.

Make the leap from local to global standards—Young, high-potential Chinese need to recognize that the appropriate standard measurement of success is global, not local. To do this, they need help in understanding the standards of success applied outside of China. Some good ways to do this are to send them to company offices or plants in other countries and to help them develop a network of contacts outside China to broaden their views at both the business and personal levels. The next chapter examines how you can manage and direct your staff's performance.

CHAPTER 10

Managing Your Team's Performance

Performance management—the setting, monitoring, and reviewing of performance goals—is not an easy task in any country. In China it is another key human resource function that needs careful consideration, given the cultural context. If not implemented carefully, then it becomes another source of frustration for expatriate managers.

Performance Management (Appraisal) Systems in the West

Before we look into how best to manage employee performance in the China context, we must first examine how it is handled in the West. While some aspects used in the West work equally well in China, there are some important differences.

Areas of Focus

Performance Goals—Most Western organizations use their performance management system to align people's performance goals with the organizational strategy and to establish accountability for achievements. The objectives set are the "whats" of performance management. Typically, progress toward these objectives is reviewed after six months and their achievement is evaluated after a year. Often, compensation is tied to goal achievement.

Behavioral Goals—Many Western companies also use their performance management system to clarify and set goals relative to *how* the performance objectives are achieved. Specific competencies (behaviors) that are related to achieving specific performance goals or that reflect the organization's culture are listed on each person's performance plan. People then are expected to demonstrate these competencies in meeting their objectives for the year. As with performance goals, progress toward behavioral goals is reviewed at six months, with a final evaluation at the end of the year. Attainment of competency goals is a factor in compensation and promotion decisions.

Development Goals—Many companies also encourage the setting of development goals as part of their performance management system. These goals relate to areas in which individuals either need to improve in their current jobs or desire to develop to progress in the organization. As with all other goals, they are set, reviewed, and evaluated over the course of a year.

Who Takes the Lead?

Bottom-up—The trend in Western organizations is to put responsibility for the performance management process on the individuals for whom the goals are being set. At the start of the performance year, they make tentative decisions about their goals (often based on reviewing a copy of their manager's goals). They then check these with their manager and reach a consensus. During the midyear review and again at the end of the year, employees evaluate their achievement of objectives, then check their evaluations with their manager and negotiate final ratings. This system can be characterized as a "bottom-up" approach to performance management.

Top-down—The alternative is the traditional "top-down" system that has been common for generations. In this system, goals are suggested by the manager, discussed, and agreed upon by the direct report. The same process is used when ratings for goal achievement are considered.

Discussion about the acceptability, problems, and advantages of these Western performance management variables—both traditional top-down and bottom-up approaches—in a Chinese setting comprises the remainder of this chapter.

Why Performance Management Is Difficult in China

Understanding how performance management traditionally has been handled in Chinese companies helps to explain the vast gap between what has been the norm and what is now required.

Historically, state-owned enterprises did not have performance management systems. Job roles and seniority dictated the pay and welfare benefits that employees received. Performance management systems have been in place in some private Chinese enterprises, but these are mostly bureaucratic, paper-pushing processes run by the personnel department. Most Chinese managers have not yet had experience using performance management as a management tool.

A Major Paradigm Shift

Lui Fen has just made a career change from a well-known private Chinese company to a foreign company. She is young and feels that she can risk making this bold move. Her new company has a Western performance management system in place, and this is her first experience with such a process. She has attended a three-hour briefing about the system, and now she realizes how very different it is from what she experienced at her former organization, as described below:

Performance Management in a Traditional Chinese Enterprise

Aspects	Description
Performance goals are static.	HR department issues a job description, which includes roles, responsibilities, and outputs of each key position. Then, each employee writes his or her performance goals based on the job description. Lui had the same set of performance goals for several years.
No measurable performance goals.	There is no strict requirement to set measurable goals. The so-called "goals" are mostly activity statements.
Personal attributes are evaluated.	A set of broad personal attributes (e.g., "loyalty," "conscientiousness," "hard-working") is used to evaluate the "quality" of the employee.
Ritually done at year's end.	The HR department sends out the performance management form at the end of each year. The manager completes the appraisal and then asks for the employee's endorsement with a signature. The form is then returned to HR for filing.

Cultural Differences That Do Not Support Performance Management

There are cultural factors in China that run counter to the basic philosophy and concepts of a Western-style performance management system. Knowing these cultural barriers will prepare you to modify aspects of your organization's performance management system for the China context:

- Accountability is a difficult concept to understand.
- Egalitarianism is preferred over recognition of performance.
- There is a lack of confidentiality about personnel decisions.
- Qualitative measures are not easily understood.
- Ethics are a problem.
- Managers are reluctant to communicate and handle performance problems.

Accountability is a difficult concept to understand—There is no direct translation of "being accountable" in the Chinese language. The closest translation is "taking responsibility." Thus, it cannot be taken for granted that your Chinese employees will understand the concept. Expatriate managers who are new to China and who do not yet understand the intricacies of the concept of accountability there often are puzzled by why work and other tasks don't get done, despite the fact that roles and performance standards are clear.

Chinese culture defines responsibility in a narrow sense. Local employees tend to accept accountability for areas they see as being within their responsibility but not for gray areas between individuals or teams. Chinese managers like to stay within their own boundary; crossing it would mean going beyond their job and upsetting the balance or harmony of the group. The results might not be delivered, but Chinese managers will not see that as their fault. A job is well done if the right process is followed. If the desired outcome is reached, then that is a happy coincidence. Chinese middle managers' lack of preparedness to accept accountability for results is one of the greatest frustrations for expatriate managers in China today.

On the other hand, Westerners define taking accountability as seizing the initiative to remove all related barriers to deliver the required results. This involves following through to ensure results. There might be areas not strictly under a Westerner's responsibility, but because he or she feels accountable for the results, the person assumes those areas as his or her own responsibility.

Also, Westerners interpret decision-making authority as having full ownership of the task: A general goal is set and the employee is free, within procedural guidelines, to plan how to achieve it and then to execute the necessary actions. In contrast, even the best of Chinese managers display reluctance to assume ownership for fear of making the wrong decision. In many cases, Chinese managers continuously delay a tough decision until it becomes critical. But in the view of expatriate managers, a few "bad" decisions are permissible as long as appropriate decision-making steps are followed.

Related to this is the challenge of getting Chinese managers to assume roles that require horizontal integration. The fear of cutting across other managers' boundaries and authority often prohibits their initiative. They know clearly that authority and power are important to their peers and particularly to their senior Chinese leaders. They will not want to risk upsetting others' power and authority, even if that is an essential part of getting results. Much work and effort will be needed to instill a culture of accountability in your organization in China.

Who Is Accountable?

Scenario 1—A new company is having a temporary cash flow shortage, so the local Chinese manager decides to withhold office rental payments for two months. He then uses the newly available cash to reimburse staff traveling expenses that were incurred during a marketing event the previous month. The expatriate manager learns of these decisions after the fact.

Who is accountable? It depends on whom you ask. The Chinese manager feels accountable only for the interests of his staff. According to him, it is the company's responsibility to take care of the financial commitments to its vendors and suppliers. But the expatriate manager thinks the Chinese manager is accountable for solving the entire problem, thinking he should have alerted headquarters about the need for more money. Because the rent is two months' late, the company might now be subject to legal threats from the landlord.

Scenario 2—An organization is developing a new line of business that will require a heavier workload. The local Chinese manager who is in charge of the new business immediately requests an increase in staffing. His boss, an expatriate manager, declines the request, believing that the extra work can be absorbed by the existing team if members work smarter and reprioritize. The Chinese manager feels he needs to protect his team from being overworked; the expatriate manager sees the Chinese manager as being accountable for achieving profitability with the minimal required resources.

Summary—Relative to accountability, there is no alignment between the expatriate manager and Chinese manager in either scenario. Accountability must be clearly defined and illustrated by examples in performance-planning meetings and during regular coaching sessions. Otherwise, there will be a continual mismatch of expectations that will lead to frustration and, eventually, a breakdown in trust.

Egalitarianism is preferred over recognition of performance—Promotions and rewards based on achievement run counter to the socialist philosophy espoused during the Communist era. Also, the traditional Chinese desire for harmony does not particularly agree with differentiation among people based on their performance.

Differentiating between individual performers and creating a culture of performance recognition are challenges for many Chinese managers. The ideal scenario from the employees' point of view is for outstanding performers to be rewarded at a higher level and for low or average performers not to be penalized. Compensating outstanding performance (when the desired result has been achieved) makes good business sense, but the Chinese also see compensation merely for hard work as "just" or fair. Nonetheless, seniority of service is the key factor in determining compensation. In the Chinese view, long-serving employees should be paid more and protected. For example, a young sales representative may have better sales numbers, but regardless of his performance, his compensation should be lower than those salespeople who have been with the company longer. At the end of each year, some Chinese companies pay a lump sum to each employee as a bonus. This amount is budgeted and is given regardless of the company's financial results for the year. Also, salary increases tend to be a set percentage for every employee and are usually linked to consumer price inflation.

In traditional Chinese companies, where management takes a paternalistic role, the form of compensation is tightly tied to welfare and benefits. The base pay of some Chinese companies is lower than foreign-owned companies, but the system of non-financial benefits is far more comprehensive. For example, employees are entitled to free meals, transportation, clothing allowances, and festival red packet *(hong bao)* money. Also, subsidized housing or company quarters are provided for long-serving employees.

The sentiment for egalitarianism is stronger among older employees for several reasons:
- Differentiating rewards based on performance results creates imbalance and, thus, disharmony.
- Hard work is respected and should be rewarded irrespective of its results. Effort, not outcome, is seen as the appropriate measure of an employee's worthiness.
- In traditional Chinese culture, management should be based on perceived fairness, first; business logic, second; and rules and discipline, third.

Younger Chinese employees are less resistant to performance-based management systems. They want to get ahead—and the sooner, the better. They tend to prefer an open system with clear performance standards so they can compete with others on a level playing field.

There is a lack of confidentiality about personnel decisions—Expatriate managers in China soon learn that nothing is truly confidential. Chinese employees exchange information among themselves about pay and performance ratings. This reflects their ambition as well as their strong need for peer comparison. Older employees are accustomed to the "open" system in state-owned enterprises where everyone knows what everyone else earns, including the managers.

Qualitative measures are not easily understood—Chinese employees might not welcome *quantitative* measurements, but they understand them. Many find *qualitative* measures, however, difficult to understand. Examples might include the quality aspects of a job or the evaluation of behavior against corporate values (discussed in Chapter 6). Expatriate managers become frustrated when performance they consider to be below standard is seen as well above standard by their Chinese employees. Often this derives from the employees' misunderstanding of the job's qualitative measures. The best solution seems to be setting very clear goals for the employees and providing plenty of examples to illustrate the different levels of qualitative measurement.

Ethics are a problem—Although the rule of law in China is weak, it is currently being strengthened considerably to be more consistent with Western standards. Still, corruption pervades many aspects of commercial life in China. Chinese would agree that we should all behave ethically and with integrity. The difficulty lies in the definition. For example, to the Chinese, large gifts (i.e., expensive items), entertainment, special privileges, or cash rebates *(hong bao)* do not constitute bribery.

Even if your employees understand your company's ethics code, they might tell you that suppliers or other stakeholders in a particular transaction expect the China way of "reciprocal" personal benefits or gains in the form of *hong bao* red packet money or special privileges. They will tell you that if the custom is not followed, the business deal might be in jeopardy.

Nevertheless, there are still multinational companies in China that vigorously uphold their ethics policy according to Western standards. One multinational pharmaceutical company terminated more than 50 staff members in three years for violating its ethics code. The company has a zero-tolerance policy when it comes to violating company ethics on rebates and bribery, large gifts, and entertainment. It sees integrity as essential to its success and acts accordingly. While not all companies are as strict, it is important that they have a clearly delineated ethics code for all to follow.

In general, in many multinationals the full implementation of an ethics policy is still a work in progress and will remain a challenge in the foreseeable future.

Managers are reluctant to communicate and handle performance problems—Delays in handling performance issues are common to managers throughout the world, but they are even more common in China. In most cases the preference in China is to actually avoid confronting poor performance issues. Nobody wants to be the messenger of bad news, especially given the need to preserve face and harmony. This means that when a situation finally becomes intolerable and must be confronted, it often comes as a surprise to the employee, leading to resentment and bitterness.

Performance Management in China: Not Nipping Problems in the Bud

Emmy has been with the company for five years. This year, much to her dismay, she was rated as one of the lowest performers in her department. This rating came as a shock, especially after she had been rated as an "outstanding" performer in her first and second years and as "successful" in her third and fourth years.

Emmy is strong-willed and aggressive when it comes to delivering results. For her first two years, she made a significant contribution, mostly working on her own. Emmy's abrasiveness was noticed, but her manager gave her no feedback about it. In Emmy's mind, her drive and assertiveness were key to her success; little else mattered.

The company has a history of promoting people based on their past performance without evaluating their skills against the requirements of the new position. And so, during her third year, Emmy was promoted to team leader, responsible for a group of five people.

In her new job Emmy had to rely on her team to achieve results; she couldn't accomplish them by herself.   The new position also had complex interdependencies with other teams; collaboration and strong partnerships with many other internal and external parties were required.

Emmy's lack of interpersonal skills and abrasive behavior caused a lot of tension with her peers and team members. Two team members quit and another openly confronted Emmy about her leadership style. Emmy was unaware that her abrasiveness was a problem.

After her fifth year with the company, Emmy was rated a low performer during her annual appraisal. She received this news from her manager's boss, not from her direct supervisor. Emmy was caught completely off guard by the feedback; she had never been told that her abrasiveness was having such a detrimental impact on her performance and career. Now she feels humiliated, confused, and angry.

How to Install a Performance Management System in China

As stated previously, making a performance management system work in China is a challenge. Doing so requires a systematic, comprehensive approach for driving the necessary cultural change. To build the basics of a performance culture, you need solid pillars strong enough to hold the roof—that is, your company's vision and ongoing business—and to weather the winds and rain—the forces that impede change, such as cultural factors, past habits, and lack of positive models. In establishing these pillars, you are building the infrastructure for the long-term success of your China team.

A strong performance management system has five pillars:

1. Operationalize the strategic direction into performance goals.
2. Provide training on performance management skills.
3. Model performance management skills.
4. Recognize achievement by using the performance management system as a basis for all human resource decisions.
5. Use a performance management system to help maintain ethics and organizational values.

Each of these pillars is examined in detail in the rest of this chapter.

1. Operationalize the strategic direction into performance goals.

For companies operating in China, success depends not so much on having a clear strategy and plan, but on how well that strategy is executed. Three things must happen to ensure successful execution:

- **Translate the organizational strategy into an actionable performance plan with clear, measurable objectives and milestones.** The managers who report to you can then develop their own objectives and milestones based on your objectives, and each level below them can do the same. In this way the performance of everyone in your unit is aligned with the organization's strategy.

- **Ensure that employees understand the importance of their contributions.** Ambitious, young Chinese employees need to know what contribution they are making to the overall success of the company. Without such knowledge, they are likely to leave.

- **Confirm that employees are clear about the evaluation standards for their objectives.** This is a prerequisite for managing Chinese employees' high expectations. They must know the criteria for their rewards, business titles, and promotions. Unclear standards will lead to differing perceptions between foreign managers and Chinese employees regarding their performance and readiness for advancement.

Older Chinese employees will have very little or no experience with a performance management system if they have worked only in Chinese enterprises. These older employees will be anxious about and perhaps resistant to setting goals. They might see measurable performance goals as limiting their job autonomy. Many will be hesitant to accept that aligning and translating the business direction into measurable goals can actually help employees to execute those goals.

To make the goal-setting process work in your China company, the strong sense of hierarchy can be leveraged to attain goal alignment. The leader–follower culture can be harnessed to ensure commitment and discipline in executing the performance management system. You can do this by ensuring that your key Chinese managers know and are committed to the goal-setting techniques, are role models in setting and reviewing goals, and are able to instruct their followers in the techniques.

Many younger Chinese employees will welcome goal setting. With clear performance targets, they will be able to demonstrate their ability to the boss and thereby advance their career. However, many organizations recognize that successfully implementing a goal-setting process with this generation means starting slowly. Employees need to be adequately trained in the necessary interaction skills in order to have meaningful, "participative" discussions.

Starting Slowly

As a leader, do not assume that installing a bottom-up approach to performance management will be easy with the younger Chinese generation. Several leaders have shared that younger Chinese employees, when given too much latitude in setting their performance goals, have embraced a "me" philosophy that has eventually led to an "employee versus the company" discussion with their manager.

One older Chinese leader at a multinational corporation that tried a bottom-up approach commented on how the younger generation seemed to take advantage of the expatriates by using the goal-setting meetings as personal negotiations to lower the leaders' expectations of them. After the initial implementation, that organization finally found success by gradually introducing the concept of employees' creating their own performance goals. Now, its leaders start performance goal-setting discussions using a top-down approach; as these discussions progress, the leaders encourage a more "participative" dialog based on their employees' openness to the approach.

The top-down approach to performance management fits the strong Chinese sense of hierarchy, whereby managers set their direct reports' goals without much negotiation. Followers are required to accept the goals. Employees might have concerns or doubts about whether new, more ambitious goals are realistic or achievable, but they will follow the order from the "commander." But even with the top-down approach, managers should involve direct reports in defining how their success will be measured. The top-down approach has the downside of blocking the upward flow of ideas from employees.

Additional training will be necessary if you want to move to a more "participative" culture that requires managers to get employees' commitment to and ownership of goals while encouraging a steady flow of ideas from the bottom.

2.　Provide training on performance management skills.

Training is essential for a well-functioning performance management system. Managers need it, as do their direct reports at all levels. Training should cover skills in setting goals, coaching, tracking performance results, and participating in performance reviews.

Performance management training is not a quick fix. Don't expect your Chinese managers to learn the requisite skills in one session. In fact, you might need to provide performance management training as a series of courses that are delivered as needed—for example, immediately before goals are set, progress is checked, and goals are evaluated.

Training on goal setting—Managers at all levels must learn how to write good, "SMART" (i.e., Specific, Measurable, Actionable, Realistic, and Time-bound) goals. Whether the system is top-down or bottom-up, the people involved must be able to write their goals so that others can understand them. Similarly, measurement methods must be understood and agreed upon.

Training on tracking performance—Part of setting actionable goals is deciding how to measure their achievement, not only at the end of the year, but during the interim. Whether the system is top-down or bottom-up, it is important that people can measure their progress. Further, it is crucial that their leaders are able to monitor their probability of goal attainment and take appropriate remedial action, such as providing additional coaching or allocating resources, if it looks like their direct reports won't be able to meet their goals. Positive reinforcement for those individuals who are on track provides encouragement and motivation.

Training on appraisal skills—In the top-down method, the annual performance appraisal discussion is often a feared event because direct reports have no idea what their manager will tell them. They often haven't received much feedback during the year, and they aren't sure how their efforts have been perceived or if they have even been noticed. In the bottom-up approach, there is much less anxiety, because the first draft of the year-end appraisal form is completed by the individual. Some insights offered by the leader might come as a surprise, but on the whole, the discussion is a lot less frightening. Either way, the ratings should be thoroughly discussed and agreed upon. You don't want the Chinese employee to simply shake his or her head, say "OK," and walk out.

Setting Performance Goals for the First Time

Deng Hong has just attended training for setting performance goals. His boss has set up a meeting with him to discuss his performance goals for this year. Deng is anxious; this is his first time to set performance goals with an expatriate manager. Deng's current job is his third since graduation. In his two previous companies, performance management was not taken seriously. But now, Deng has had performance management training conducted by HR staff from headquarters. He found the training useful, as it provided him with a solid understanding about how the process will work along with some specific skills and experience on identifying key result areas, setting performance goals, and measuring performance. Although he is looking forward to the meeting with his manager, he is anxious just the same.

To start the meeting, Ray, his manager, tells Deng that he has reserved one full hour for the discussion. Ray makes a point to switch his cell phone to silent mode, and then explains the purpose of the meeting and the proposed agenda.

The meeting unfolds as follows, with Ray taking the lead:

> Ray shows his own performance goals to Deng and explains that he discussed them with his boss at the head office two weeks ago. Ray also highlights how important it is for them to achieve this year's goals because China is one of the key growth markets in the company's global expansion plan.

> Using the template provided by headquarters, Ray explains and discusses the elements in each part of the goal-setting system. The template is the same as the one used in Deng's training.

> Ray takes examples of his own performance goals and asks Deng how they can be translated to Deng's current job and this year's performance goals.

> Ray then discusses the behavioral competencies required to meet the goals and how the company's values might affect them.

> Together, they decide on Deng's development goals for the year.

Ray pauses to check for Deng's understanding every few minutes and to make sure the discussion is two-way. Ray proceeds slowly as he notices Deng diligently taking notes. He sees that Deng is trying to absorb each piece of information.

Before Ray closes the meeting, he asks Deng how he feels about this process. Deng is almost speechless; he had not expected his manager to ask him this question so directly. He politely responds that he appreciates his manager's time and commitment to have such an involved discussion with him. Privately, Deng feels more than grateful; this is the first time in his career that he has had such a meaningful performance discussion with any of his leaders.

Deng agrees to document the discussion and use the template provided by headquarters to complete crafting his performance, behavioral, and development goals by the end of the week.

Deng walks out of his manager's office feeling great relief. The meeting was mentally and psychologically demanding, but was worth it. He now has a much better understanding of Ray's expectations regarding his performance. The meeting confirms that his decision to join the company was a good one, although so far, both the stress and stretch have been much more than in his previous jobs.

3. Model performance management skills.

Getting a bottom-up or top-down performance management system to work requires managers at each level to have and use performance management skills. In best-practice organizations worldwide, modeling the skills starts at the top and cascades down throughout the organization. Performance management is a difficult concept to convey in words, particularly from one language to another. It is best encouraged through practical modeling by higher-level managers.

It is important to set clear expectations about what will happen if subordinate managers fail to set performance goals with their reports. Chinese tend to accept rules within the family, in schools, and in society more generally. If the understanding is established that goals will be set, reviewed in six months, and then evaluated annually, then the people who report to you will generally follow through. Those who do not comply will need to understand the penalty for noncompliance—perhaps in the form of a deferred training opportunity or overseas trip or by way of a short-term reduction in financial rewards. Certainly, in most Western companies, managers' success in executing the performance management system is one of their performance objectives.

All performance management systems must be audited periodically to ensure they are being implemented properly. Requiring staff to fill out forms is one thing, but getting them to do a good job of setting goals and then reviewing them is quite another. A good rule of thumb is for an organization to audit 10 percent of the performance management forms submitted by its managers, and then provide feedback to the managers and their bosses on the forms' completeness and quality.

Follow Through on Poor Performers, but Be Sensitive
In China it is a cultural prerequisite to provide poor performers with ample opportunity to redeem themselves before taking disciplinary measures. That the manager gives the employee a chance to reform is an important gesture in keeping with traditional Chinese values. Thus, it is recommended that you strictly adhere to a three-stage approach for exiting poor performers:

- **Stage 1**—Give a verbal warning and set up a performance improvement plan for the individual. It should include an action plan, milestones, and means of measurement so that the employee has a clear path to follow.

- **Stage 2**—Employees who do not improve their performance should get a warning that clearly states the consequences for continued failure to meet standards. For example, someone might be redeployed to a job with lesser skill requirements to give him or her more of a chance to turn around the poor performance.

- **Stage 3**—If the employee's performance remains unsatisfactory, he or she should be asked to resign to save face. Employers must pay severance compensation according to applicable labor laws; otherwise, legal claims can arise.

Such a phased approach for moving poor performers out of the company need not occur over years. In China the process can be completed in 10 to 15 months. The employee who is facing disciplinary action can be reviewed in shorter performance cycles—possibly once every three months. The performance review schedules and possible disciplinary outcomes should be clearly laid out in written documents. During this process the manager and company need to be seen as fair, supportive, and sensitive.

A manager's patience and support during this course of action can actually lead to the employee's gratitude. For example, a manager can help an employee save face by saying the individual is leaving for family reasons.

Some multinational companies and Chinese private enterprises handle poor performers with far greater speed and candor than the process just described. But mostly they are high-tech companies populated with young, educated employees and have a culture of speed and immediate high performance. Employees in such organizations expect to be dealt with quickly. Also, most will not want to waste time if there is a mismatch of skills or expectations.

Probationary Periods and Employment Contracts

Most professionals are hired in China under an employment contract that can range from one to three years. For most professional staff (e.g., sales representatives, engineers, and office staff), the common contract length is three years. Generally, university graduates expect a three-year contract.

The contract length will determine the span of the probationary period. According to Chinese labor law,[1] employment contracts beyond three months and less than one year have a probationary period of one month. Employment contracts between one and three years have a probationary period that can be extended to two months; for employment contracts longer than three years, probation can last up to six months. The length of the probationary period is very important, because during this time employment can be terminated without "proven" reasons and without severance payments. All the organization needs to do is communicate to the employee why there is a mismatch between the individual and the company. It does not have to provide evidence of poor performance. If the employee is terminated after the probationary period expires, the organization must provide proven reasons for the termination along with severance pay.

Too many Western companies in China fail to take advantage of the probationary period to sever their relationship with poorly performing individuals. Doing so is particularly important because the difficulty of obtaining accurate reference checks (as discussed in Chapter 4) makes it easier for poor performers to slip through the hiring process. Some companies literally have no process to evaluate people a month before their probationary period expires to determine if they would be a good ongoing investment for the organization. Smarter organizations schedule a performance review one month before the probationary period ends so they can make appropriate judgments.

Similarly, some organizations schedule a performance evaluation near the end of the employment contract (e.g., three years after hiring), when Chinese employees can opt not to renew their contract. If so, they are not entitled to severance pay. If the company chooses not to renew the contract, it must provide a severance payment according to the law, but it does not have to give reasons for the decision not to continue the person's employment. Savvy expatriate managers mark their calendars to check that there are no problems before an employee signs a new contract. They review the individual's completed performance management forms and ask for specific examples of good and poor performance or attitude.

When it is appropriate to terminate an employee during the term of the performance contract, the company must be prepared to show cause and pay severance. Having well-documented performance management records showing that measurable goals were not reached, along with records of warnings and offers of help, are invaluable in limiting severance payments.

4. Recognize achievement by using the performance management system as a basis for all human resource decisions.

An effective performance management system does little good unless it is used. It makes no sense to spend time and money establishing the system and then not using it to assign people to jobs, make promotion decisions, guide pay raises, and determine job titles, compensation, and training opportunities, including who will be assigned overseas training and who will attend external conferences.

Relying on performance management data as one of the main criteria in making a range of HR decisions reinforces the system's importance. It also bolsters the fairness of decisions based on the system. As mentioned, the perception of fairness is a big part of managing performance in China.

Managers in China often are tempted to make exceptions to the performance management system, particularly for people whom they are very eager to retain. When an individual who is not performing as well as others gets a promotion or some other form of recognition, management is sending a message to the employees that factors other than performance influence such decisions. Such a practice is short-sighted; the organization might save one or two people, but it risks losing high performers who might feel inadequately recognized.

Also, the link between compensation and performance results must be applied consistently. Inconsistency in this area can lead to problems. For example: At year one, a manager decides against reducing an employee's bonus even though the person has not been performing up to the required target. The manager is being "generous" by giving the employee a second chance— something that is communicated to the person in the hope that it will be taken as a motivational message. At year two, the person performs better, but is still behind target, so the manager decides to reduce the performance bonus. The employee threatens to resign. In his eyes, his bonus has been reduced even though his sales results have improved.

5. Use a performance management system to help maintain ethics and organizational values.

In addition to specific job objectives, performance management systems in China must cover organizational values. You do not want people achieving their goals in an unethical or dishonest way. In China it is even more important than in the West that an organization's values are clearly enunciated to its employees. Basic values of honesty and ethics need to be converted to job-related behavioral terms as well. A Western company might not have honesty stated explicitly as a company value, but most likely it is an implicit value. In China, however, honesty must be specifically required and defined. For example, sales staff must know that they cannot promise or imply that products will accomplish tasks beyond those defined in the product specifications.

Disciplinary action should be taken if company rules or ethics are violated, and employment can be terminated for serious transgressions. But the rules must be clearly laid out beforehand. Terminations based on vague, unwritten rules could land an employer in a labor tribunal. If there is any ambiguity in the company's rules, then such tribunals tend to find in favor of the dismissed employee. Best practices in this area include ensuring that employee handbooks and guidelines are up to date and devoid of ambiguity, and ensuring that company values are built into the performance management system.

Remember: Just because a company chooses to operate in China does not mean that it needs to or should change its ethical standards. But clear guidelines are required to cover all contingencies with regard to donations, entertainment, gifts to and from vendors and other outside parties, samples to clients, and compliance with intellectual property protection laws.

Setting Ethics Requirements Higher Than the Social Norm

A local employee was caught cheating on a professional qualification examination administered by a U.S. company. The employee was terminated based on a clearly stated company policy that behaving dishonestly would result in immediate termination. Compared to China norms, this is a stringent standard. Normally, if local Chinese were found to have been dishonest in such an external examination, they would lose only their right to continue that exam. They could apply for another certification at a later time.

The U.S. company decided to pursue a higher standard because of its belief that "integrity" should not be compromised. It was the company's decision to make.

Modeling Performance Management

This chapter has examined many of the complexities of performance management, which is one of the most difficult tasks you will face as an expatriate manager in China. Very quickly you come up against cultural traditions and norms that work against what you need to achieve. But managing performance is integral to being a successful manager. It is one of the criteria against which your own performance will be judged. You need to create an environment that is fair, that rewards those who should be rewarded, and that upholds the company's standards and ethics. You must have clearly enunciated, comprehensive rules that will help you be seen as a fair, trustworthy, predictable, and consistent leader. Your modeling of performance management will be an important step in the education of China's future leaders.

CHAPTER 11

Growing Ready Local Leaders

I t is not uncommon to hear that a multinational corporation has a five-year strategy in China to increase revenue by $3 billion, which in turn requires hundreds of additional general managers to drive the business. Nor is it uncommon to hear that an organization plans to triple the size of its China management team. The headlines look good, the share price goes up, and the stockholders are happy. The difficulty comes when it is time for an organization to reconcile such plans with reality. And the operational reality is that most multinational corporations do not have the ready leaders to manage their accelerating businesses. Most understand that local leadership is the linchpin for their China operation's future success. But the shortage of good leaders in China means that CEOs and executives are overstretched; ideas and opportunities might abound, but there's insufficient leadership talent for their execution.

One strategy to compensate for the lack of qualified local leaders is to fill the gap with expatriate managers. And thus, as the economy grows, so does the number of foreigners working in China. By the end of 2006, the number of new expatriates who had applied for China work permits reached a record high of more than 180,000. This is double the number of people with permits in 2003, according to figures from the China Ministry of Labor and Social Security.[1] The number of expatriates who traveled frequently to China is much higher than this. In 2006 Shanghai, China's bustling financial center, employed more than 54,000 foreign workers, with a majority in some sort of a leadership role.[2] However, expatriates are not the best solution for most organizations that are seeking to create a sustainable, profitable business.

There are several disadvantages to filling the leadership gap with expatriates. Cost is a significant one. Typically, an expatriate assigned to China costs up to five times his or her salary. Also, few are fully aware of the cultural nuances of the China market. Another disadvantage is that the presence of expatriates limits the opportunities for local employees to take on greater responsibilities in running the organization's business, which is referred to as localization.

Localization takes many forms in China. One localization strategy is to formulate a clear plan as to when all or most of the expatriates will be replaced by local Chinese managers. Another strategy is to hold the number of expatriate manager positions constant and then fill newly created positions with local managers. This would allow for certain critical positions (e.g., finance director) to be exempted. Such a plan is acceptable to the Chinese employees if it is clearly enunciated. Secret or vague plans fuel perceptions that there remains a "glass ceiling" for local managers, and as stated previously, this can lead to turnover of valuable people.

Some multinational companies do have grand plans for localizing their management in China, but these plans typically originate from the head office. For example, the headquarters of one organization gave the directive not to replace any expatriates once their contracts expired. Another head office set an objective that 80 percent of its senior management must be local within three years. But most organizations lack the direction and capability to meet such goals. So what is the on-the-ground solution? Companies must grow their own local leaders!

But how do you grow your own leaders in China? Where do you start, and how do you focus your energy? When building a leadership pipeline in a fast-paced, growing economy, where do you focus your organization's development investment to receive the greatest value? How do you optimize your talent by identifying high potentials, assessing their readiness for the next level, and ensuring that their development happens? Answers to these questions are covered in this chapter.

Leadership Pipelines and Acceleration Pools®

Finding and keeping quality local, high-potential talent is the number one obstacle facing multinational corporations in China. Although high-performing employees leave if they are not promoted, there is a danger that if they are promoted too soon, they will fail.

Two strategies, described in detail below, will succeed in developing the leaders that organizations need:

- A leadership pipeline that provides needed talent at each management level.
- An Acceleration Pool® that will hasten the development of a few people for senior positions when there is no time to move them up slowly in the leadership pipeline.

Building a Leadership Pipeline

In a leadership pipeline strategy, leaders at each organizational level are developed within the limits of their capacity and motivation so that each year their performance (and thus, their contribution to the organization) improves. How this development occurs has been examined in previous chapters. A pipeline strategy also means that a few select people are groomed for the next level of management through special training, job experiences, and coaching. Not all jobs are the same at any given level in terms of their development potential. Some will provide a wider range of experiences or contacts; some will provide more job challenges. Also, some managers are better at developing people than others. It is very important that these growth positions go to the people who will benefit most—the people with the highest potential for the next level. An important responsibility of the expatriate manager is to see that this happens.

Checking Up on the Pipeline

One multinational corporation in China conducts a biannual workforce review to understand where it needs to focus its attention (i.e., determine where the pipeline is the weakest). In this process, business leaders and their HR partners discuss their business unit's (or department's) strategies and workforce implications. Capability gaps are examined, and a talent supply risk analysis is conducted that focuses on the quality of bench strength, probable attrition, new positions, future leaders' time to develop, expatriate contract expirations, localization requirements, and so on for each leadership level.

> The output of these reviews serves a dual function: It facilitates a business unit's strategic workforce action plan, and it highlights the most critical leadership levels for attention, which prioritizes the HR department's efforts on talent-development initiatives.

Building an Acceleration Pool®

For most fast-growing organizations in China, the progression of individuals through the leadership pipeline to their eventual top positions takes too long in terms of organizational needs and the expectations of the best local leaders at each level. There needs to be some way to fast-track those special few people with the capacity and motivation to rise to the top relatively quickly. An Acceleration Pool® provides such a fast track.

Acceleration Pools (also known as high-potential pools or high-flyer pools) operate independently of the leadership pipeline. Pool members receive special training and mentoring in order to accelerate their development. Most of all, they get the very best assignments, enabling them to stretch their skills and show what they can do. The concept of and need for an Acceleration Pool is described in detail in *Grow Your Own Leaders.* The following sidebar replicates key points of an Acceleration Pool system from *Grow Your Own Leaders.*[3]

Acceleration Pools

In traditional replacement-planning systems, senior and middle managers identify potential successors for themselves (and sometimes for their direct reports) and estimate when those individuals will be ready to move up the organizational ladder. From these inputs the HR department develops a series of charts showing the backups for each position and their readiness. Positions with no backups are identified, and meetings are held to fill the open slots on the charts. That process can consume an inordinate amount of time, with relatively little gain. One major U.S. company discovered that it was devoting 250,000 executive hours a year to completing and discussing replacement-planning forms.

As a rule, companies don't get much of a return on that time investment. Replacement-planning systems are often out of touch with organizational strategies because executives are essentially looking to replace themselves. That is, they are looking for people to do the same things they are doing in their current jobs. However, this could be at a time when the company might be rolling out a new strategy that requires an executive with much different knowledge and competencies, or the organization might even be eliminating the executive's job completely. In addition, there is usually very little focus on skill development, as most of the attention is concentrated on job placement. But worst of all, the majority of actual replacement decisions are made outside the replacement-planning system. Most organizations that have done formal research on their replacement-planning process have determined their designated backups actually fill fewer than 30 percent of the open positions for which they were slotted. Thus, companies are spending large chunks of executive time on a system that is not used when needed.

Acceleration Pools represent a drastic departure from traditional replacement planning. Rather than targeting one or two hand-picked people for each specific executive position, an Acceleration Pool develops a group of high-potential candidates for executive jobs in general. As the name implies, the development of these pool members is accelerated through stretch job and task force assignments that offer the best learning and highest-visibility opportunities. Pool members have an assigned mentor, receive more training, and attend special developmental experiences, such as university executive programs and in-house action learning sessions. They also get more feedback and coaching. With the help of the HR department, senior management actively tracks pool members' development and readiness.

In an Acceleration Pool system, senior executives no longer need to worry about deciding who is going to back up whom in their organization, except for the top positions. The annual chore of completing replacement-planning forms is eliminated, which gives executives more time to focus on skills and knowledge development—that is, on cultivating tomorrow's leaders.

Figure 11.1: Acceleration Pool in a Midsize Company

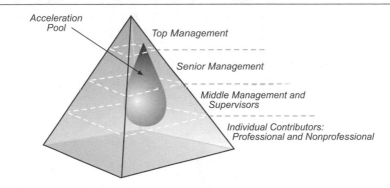

The size of an Acceleration Pool depends on the number of executive positions, the number of candidates the organization would like to choose from in filling target positions, and the speed at which the organization is growing. Figure 11.1 shows a hypothetical example of a pool that might be found in a midsize company (1,000 to 5,000 employees) preparing candidates for general management positions.

There can be many variations on the basic Acceleration Pool shown in Figure 11.1. A larger organization might have two pools—one starting at the supervisory and professional individual contributor level and one starting at the middle management level (see Figure 11.2).

Figure 11.2: Large Company with Two Acceleration Pools

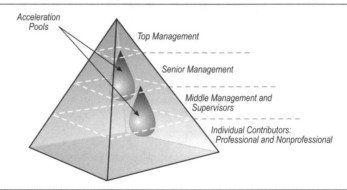

The number of pools often reflects how a company is organized. For example, an Acceleration Pool in a manufacturing organization might exist to fill top plant-management positions, while a pool of middle managers might be designated to fill a range of corporate positions. Often, large strategic business units (SBUs) will have their own Acceleration Pool to fill senior SBU positions in addition to the wider company pool that is aimed at filling senior corporate management positions (see Figure 11.3).

Figure 11.3: Organization with a Pool in Each Business Unit and a Pool for Corporate Positions

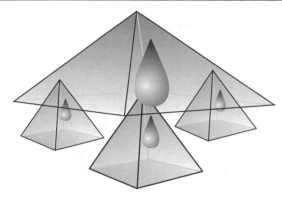

When Is the Best Time to Identify People for an Acceleration Pool?

Although an Acceleration Pool is open to people at any level or age, there usually is a typical career point or organizational level at which the majority of members enter. Management faces a quandary in defining that typical entry point: It is important to identify people early enough so that they have plenty of time for development; but the longer management waits to identify people, the more accurate the prediction of growth potential will be.

So, while there is no "absolutely right" common entry point, research data indicate that evaluations are more accurate when people have been in work situations for a few years and less accurate when performed on those just entering the organization from a university or some other background.

With the speed of growth in China, many companies might feel that they lack the luxury of waiting several years before inviting good staff into their Acceleration Pools. In this case they might find that admitting people earlier is a business necessity. Based on DDI's work establishing Acceleration Pools in China, we believe pool candidates should have a minimum of one year working experience within a company before they can be considered as "high potential." Any sooner, and the organization will experience difficulty evaluating the individual's "true" growth potential and end up spending considerable development investment (i.e., time and money) on the wrong people.

Identifying High Potentials for Accelerated Development in China

Once organizations in China realize that their current senior management bench strength is not sufficient, they need to scan their talent at all levels to see which individuals have the highest potential to grow into senior leaders. They can then go about constructing their own Acceleration Pool.

Many employers in China make the following two mistakes when identifying high potentials:

Mistake 1: Focusing on current performance—not management potential.
Many times when an organization is asked how it identifies high potentials, the response is simply that it is left to the managers' own judgment. This is a big mistake. Justifying the difference between "high performer" and "high potential" can be tricky, even in Western cultures, because many managers confuse "performance" with "potential." Most Chinese managers identify potential based on a person's current strong performance along with some of their own biases (his or her schoolmates, relationships, family ties, etc.) and gut instincts. But individuals who are competent or even strong in their current job may not perform well at higher levels. For example, your best salesperson might not make a good sales executive. Naturally, an individual's sustained business performance should be considered, but not exclusively. It is necessary to strike a balance and complement evaluations of "performance" with evaluations of "potential."

Through its extensive experience and research over three decades of working with organizations to identify and develop leaders, DDI has identified 10 leadership potential factors. (See Figure 11.4.)

Figure 11.4: DDI's Leadership Potential Factors[4]

Leadership Promise

► **Propensity to Lead**
► **Brings Out the Best in People**
► **Authenticity**

Balance of Values and Results

► **Culture Fit**
► **Passion for Results**

Personal Development Orientation

► **Receptivity to Feedback**
► **Learning Agility**

Mastery of Complexity

► **Adaptability**
► **Conceptual Thinking**
► **Navigates Ambiguity**

Mistake 2: Identifying candidates without subsequent diagnosis of specific development needs.

Another key mistake is overusing the data for identifying potential. Managers in one multinational corporation wondered why its high potentials were failing in their new roles. The organization had instituted an interview process and special online rating systems to identify high-potential talent. The flaw appeared when this process, which was targeted only to identify high potentials, was leveraged over the next few years to determine salary increases, make promotion decisions, and drive retention efforts. It is not uncommon for organizations in China to take full advantage of something they have purchased, sometimes to a point beyond its intended use or to the point it produces no real value. The criteria for identifying leadership potential should be intrinsically different from the criteria used to diagnose the development needs of individuals at a specific level of leadership (i.e., competencies, job challenges, knowledge, and personal attributes—the Success Profile). See Chapter 4 for more on this.

Affirming Readiness and Diagnosing Development Needs

After an organization identifies individuals for the Acceleration Pool, the next step is to establish a sound method for assessing candidates against the senior management Success Profile. An objective assessment paints a realistic, accurate picture of where individuals stand relative to the skills needed at the target leadership level. From the organization's perspective, this assessment provides senior management with an inventory of its current available talent to carry out the strategic priorities, their readiness for movement, and their development needs. From the individual's standpoint, the assessment provides a detailed diagnosis of development needs.

DDI has designed a series of assessment tools to evaluate candidates' potential to succeed at senior levels and to diagnose their development needs. Chapter 4 has a more thorough description of a DDI Acceleration Center experience.

In China demand is high for assessment in the development of high potentials. There are several reasons for this:

- Chinese high potentials have an insatiable desire to grow and develop themselves and their careers. When providing these individuals with Acceleration Center feedback, it's not unusual to hear them describe it as the first time in their career that they have received fair, direct, and constructive feedback.

- In the past, local managers often fell into the trap of assessing high potentials based on *guanxi,* or the loyalty each employee has shown to them. As one local manager once described his criteria, "I pick potential based on who will die for me."

- Internal equity and perceptions of fairness are important in the competitive arena of the Chinese workplace. Formal assessment techniques mean that all high potentials are assessed using the same tools and standards, which enables a reliable, consistent standard to be used across the organization. This puts high potentials and their sponsoring managers on the same field, minimizing favoritism and any silo mentality.

- Chinese high potentials frequently overestimate their own abilities. Formal assessment and feedback from an unbiased, third-party expert allows each person a full understanding of his or her skills as they relate to the targeted success profile.

The "day-in-the-life," one-day Acceleration Center exercise tends to be seen by young Chinese high potentials as extremely fair and valid. When designed and administered effectively, these exercises, like a flight simulator, mirror the key decisions, interactions, and strategic challenges that occur from day to day; they also reflect the ambiguous environment in which these actions take place. The experience allows participants to try on their future roles, accountabilities, and activities in a realistic, simulated business environment. Participants find that these stretch experiences deliver well-rounded insights about their strengths and development needs and give them a realistic job preview. One China high potential who participated in a DDI assessment commented afterward that he had never realized that a business unit leader in his company had such a challenging, complex role.

Characteristics of High Potentials in China

High potentials in China are pragmatic, self-interested, and quick to seize new opportunities. They also are ambitious and hard working and, unlike earlier generations, are prepared to take risks. Often, young high potentials in China are viewed by their cohorts as aggressive and overly ambitious. Because of this, a common task for their mentors is to help guide them through interpersonal relationships with their colleagues and peers.

High potentials are prepared to move between unrelated industries or sectors. They understand that they are not building functional competencies, but leadership and business competencies.

Also, a high percentage of high potentials have overseas exposure—perhaps from overseas, tertiary, or post-graduate education or a foreign work assignment.

Ensuring That Development Happens

What happens after high potentials' strengths and development areas have been identified? All too often, both they and their organization fail to capitalize on the assessment feedback they have received. As a result, the identified individuals (pool members) fail to develop, improve, or become any more ready to be executives or senior leaders.

Young high potentials want to move up, attain new job titles, and move on to regional positions in Asia. They are extremely mobile and very vulnerable to the lure of competitors, as they are highly visible, prime targets of major headhunters. But growth takes time and needs the support of their manager and HR department.

Taking into consideration the often stretched, understaffed, and inexperienced available HR support and the chaotic business environment typical of many organizations, what does it take to grow your high potentials? First off, look at the pitfalls that can cause development efforts to fail, and then you will have a better understanding of several key approaches and considerations that have enabled successful execution of high potentials' development in China.

Development Failures

There are many possible reasons that a young high-potential employee would fail to develop. Here are nine that occur frequently enough to mention:

1. No written plans.
All too often, people fail to record their development plans. Instead, they try to keep a "mental" plan for their development. One expatriate manager in China put pen to paper, but then only briefly; his development plan simply stated the following on a reminder note: "Be a better coach." Lee Iacocca, former chairman of Chrysler Corporation, said, "The discipline of writing something down is the first step toward making it happen. In conversation, you can get away with all kinds of vagueness and nonsense, often without even realizing it. But there's something about putting your thoughts on paper that forces you to get down to specifics. That way, it's harder to deceive yourself—or anybody else."[5] He is right.

DDI research in the U.S. has found a strong link between having a well-thought-out, written development plan and subsequent meaningful development actions.[6] The same relationship applies in China.

2. Unattainable development objectives.

One participant in a high-potential coaching session in China insisted that his development goal was to become his company's next Asia Pacific CFO. But this person had been with the company for only two years and was then a mid-level manager in the finance department. When asked for more details about his plan, such as what skill gaps he had identified and how he intended to acquire the necessary skills, knowledge, and experiences to fill them, it became clear that the individual had no idea how to achieve his goal.

This brings into focus the second reason that development fails even though a plan is created: What is proposed is unattainable. This happens when people try to take on too much—they might set lofty goals or create a plan with four or five goals. It is better to focus on a plan with only one or two goals per year. In the course of the year, if those are accomplished, then the individual can move on to new goals.

3. Failing to focus on the total person.

Sometimes development can fall short due to a failure to focus on the total person. For example, this can happen when pool members focus only on knowledge. When auditing development plans for one organization in China, DDI found that 87 percent of the plans focused on technical knowledge and only 13 percent addressed behavior.

As mentioned in Chapter 4, all the Success Profile components (i.e., competencies, job challenges, knowledge, and personal attributes) must be considered.

4. Starting with a blank slate for development ideas.

Sometimes development fails because individuals are given a development action form (DAF) or an individual development plan (IDP), but no guidance on how to acquire their targeted skills and then apply them on the job. Time is wasted on development activities when there is little chance of skill improvement.

5. "I learn, therefore I do."

Development efforts need to plan for both the acquisition and the on-the-job application of new skills. In China it is common for employees to attend an MBA or EMBA program. But, after acquiring the knowledge, rarely is there a conscious effort to apply it immediately on the job. This means that new insights, learning, and skills often are lost.

6. Development is not related to the business.

Another common reason for failure is when personal development occurs in a vacuum. Individual development is most easily accomplished when there is alignment between the person's needs, the challenges of his or her role, and the organization's business drivers (see Figure 11.5). For example, a mid-level manager might attend an EMBA strategic-thinking course, yet not have responsibility or involvement in strategic or business planning. Without appropriate alignment, organizations can be paying for development that leads to no organizational payoff later. It also makes development more difficult because it is an effort that supplements—rather integrates with—day-to-day work.

Figure 11.5: Alignment of Development Opportunities

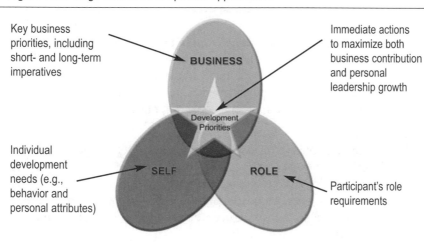

7. Failure to address multiple development opportunities with a single activity/assignment.

One development activity, if well planned, often can address a person's multiple development gaps. Figure 11.6 shows how various needs can overlap and be satisfied with one well-designed, targeted training or development intervention.

Figure 11.6: Ideal Development Opportunities

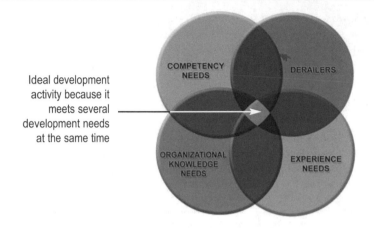

Ideal development activity because it meets several development needs at the same time

COMPETENCY NEEDS

DERAILERS

ORGANIZATIONAL KNOWLEDGE NEEDS

EXPERIENCE NEEDS

8. Managers simply "sign the check" and abdicate development.

A major roadblock to people's development in China is their boss's lack of involvement. Managers need to be involved early and often to help refine and prioritize goals, remove barriers, provide resources and support, and, in particular, seize opportunities for their people to apply their new skills on the job.

9. No metrics to show development progress.

Not only are quantitative measures of achieved job performance goals absolutely critical, but so are measures of success of development goals. Progress measures in both areas ensure continued motivation. However, for many Chinese employees, no quantitative measures of development are ever established. This makes it easy for people to delay development activities, no matter how highly motivated they are.

How Do You Develop Your High Potentials?

Organizations can plan for the challenges ahead on their high potentials' development journey once those challenges have been defined. This means having the appropriate development tools, systems, and processes in place. What is the best way to develop your Chinese high potentials? There is no hard-and-fast answer. Development takes many forms, which is a good thing because, obviously, not everyone has the same development needs or learns in the same way. For instance, while some prefer a learning approach that includes structured training or knowledge acquisition followed by on-the-job skill application, others prefer to dive into a task and learn by doing.

In some situations the choice of how to develop will be straightforward; in others, multiple options will need to be weighed to decide on the right development actions. What initiatives are useful for evaluating which development route to take in China? Establishing a development plan, careful mentoring, and job assignments and rotations are among the best options. These are discussed next.

Development Plans

High potentials and their managers, their mentors, and, often, an HR representative should partner to establish a personalized, focused development plan. The direct manager and assigned mentor should help the person refine developmental activities and line up the support needed (e.g., cooperation of another department). The ultimate success of a high potential's development and the program itself will be directly affected by the level and quality of support and the active coaching the manager provides.

Developing high-potential talent means exposing people to a range of functions and experiences and increasing their leadership and management responsibilities. Creating such opportunities is a major responsibility of top management, including expatriates. Individuals in China will be looking forward to your actions, and most will be very open to any assignments they are given. They prefer positions that:

- Raise their profile with key organizational leaders or expose them to an influential group in the community.
- Provide them with skills and experience that will bolster their value and add to the quality of their personal portfolio.
- Differentiate them from other people in the organization or marketplace.

Young high potentials need to be challenged, and providing the right level of challenge is important. It can't be too easy, or it is no challenge. Make it too hard, and it might undermine their confidence. Mentoring and coaching by the direct manager during the development process are key to preventing this from happening.

The Career Discussion in China

What questions should managers ask their high-potential employees during career discussion meetings? Here are some suggestions:

> **What strengths do you bring to the company?** This question reminds Chinese employees that they were hired to contribute to the company and that the work relationship is not entirely about their own needs. Don't assume that all high-potential employees have an accurate view of what they bring to the table. Many either have an inflated idea, or they undervalue their contribution.

> **Which direction do you want to take?** What type of work would you like to be doing in five years? Many high-potential employees jump between jobs without a clear sense of direction or a clear plan.

> **Do you want to become a business leader or a specialist?** What are your goals? Many Chinese employees aspire to reach a leadership position in the shortest possible time, but they might not have thought about the difference between being a business leader and a specialist. Some get into a managerial position only to find that their strengths and motivation are more suited to a specialist role.

> **Would you be interested in working overseas?** One recent large survey of Chinese graduates across China found that only 28 percent of the respondents wanted to work internationally. Most indicated that, while they were interested in traveling overseas for training, they did not want to live and work abroad for extended periods.[7]

> **What skills do you need to learn and practice to realize your career goals?** Many will need help to break their main career goal into smaller, more actionable goals.

> **Are you looking forward to staying with us, or are you thinking of moving elsewhere?** When there is a solid, trusting relationship between the manager and the high-potential employee, it is helpful to have the person verbally declare his or her commitment to the company. Chinese value allegiance to the leader and the team, so there is value in openly seeking a commitment from the employee to stay.

Expatriate managers do not always look forward to the career discussion process, seeing it as an occasion for tensions to arise. Instead, they should view it as a structured means to supplement or even open communication channels, reaffirm the local employee's value, and illuminate how they can contribute to the employee's career. This can minimize the scope of surprise on both sides and help to strengthen the personal bond between the manager and employee.

Mentoring in China

Mentoring is very important in the China context. Because age and experience are so respected, providing young, high-potential employees with an older, more senior mentor will be greatly appreciated by the employees.

Many expatriate managers opt for a mentoring role to ensure that their high potentials' development remains on track. Some other options include using senior Chinese managers as coaches or mentors or bringing in external coaches. Asimco Technologies, which manufactures car components, overcame its retention problems by identifying 25 up-and-coming leaders every year and assigning them mentors and specific projects. After six years, 90–95 percent of the managers initially recruited were still with the company.[8]

Another company in China experienced rapid growth and soon found that it had too few potential leaders in its pipeline. It could not afford to lose those that it did have. The CEO personally assigned four senior leaders to be mentors to the company's pool of eight young, high-potential employees. The CEO then engaged an external consultant to work with the mentoring team. The consultant began by assessing each high potential's needs and then worked with each person's boss and mentor to devise detailed, personalized development plans with documented achievement goals. The mentors were relieved to get the coaching from the outside consultant. They knew their role was important, but were unsure about how to carry it out.

Although effective mentors provide insight and guidance to their protégés, their main role is to act as a catalyst between the protégés and their respective bosses. In most cases, the boss has the opportunity to put people in learning situations, send them to training programs, and give them organizational exposure. Too often, managers accept responsibility for developing people, and while their intentions are good, they become subverted by daily work pressures. Subsequently, they pull people out of training programs, fail to follow through on commitments, and the like. Having a mentor involved who must make a biannual report to top management on an individual's progress puts considerable pressure on managers to follow through with their commitments to develop their people.

Assignments/Rotations

For most individuals seeking to maximize their development, formal training must be supplemented by structured, on-the-job assignments. For these assignments, the high potential's manager should set goals, appraise performance, and provide feedback when the job is complete. When lacking sufficient time and resources to closely monitor the development progress of a high potential in a rotational assignment, a manager might find it easy to just assume positive development is occurring. In China, where job rotations are common, managers must avoid this inclination and instead be very proactive in monitoring the person's performance and guaranteeing that the development activities have the desired impact.

Adjusting Development Programs for China

Compared with high potentials elsewhere, those in China have different expectations as learners. Generally, they prefer:
- More action learning.
- More application models and tools, and less theory.
- More links to current/future business challenges.
- A focused, business-relevant context.
- Development that is tied to results.
- Opportunity to network.
- Formation of business partnerships at different functional/operating levels.

Other Considerations for Growing Ready Chinese Leaders

What Commitments Are Required from Senior Executives?

Executives' time, commitment, and active follow-through are critical success factors to growing their high-potential talent. Senior executives' most critical roles are to:
- Articulate and communicate a clear talent strategy for the organization.
- Actively engage in the development of a talent management framework and the identification of high-potential individuals.
- Sponsor and drive the accelerated development of one or more key high potentials.
- Present and discuss high potentials' development progress with other senior executives at every possible opportunity.
- Be accountable and hold others accountable for realizing talent growth.

If your organization's executives are not embracing these roles, then you should question whether the organization is getting the full value from its efforts.

Should You Communicate the Existence of Your High-Potential Program (Acceleration Pool)?

Some companies prefer an "open" high-potential program—one that's visible for all to see and is highly formalized. Other organizations opt for more of a closed program where special development attention is given without disclosing the high-potential status of its participants to the rest of the company.

One benefit of an open program is that it reinforces high potentials' determination to succeed and reduces their motivation to look elsewhere for career growth. Such programs also make an organization attractive to other promising high potentials who see a good chance of getting into them. One multinational corporation is well known to Chinese engineers and top graduates not just for the company's brand, but also for its ability to develop mid-level managers into senior leaders. This is a major draw when the company recruits and selects potential managers.

The risk with an open development program can be the backlash of resentment and disappointment from those not selected to participate. Companies also need to guard against certain employees deliberately fostering an elitist culture, particularly given the high importance attached to status and face in China. This is where proper communication about the program's purpose, objectives, and criteria for entry can alleviate misunderstandings. In addition, the organization needs to be clear with high potentials regarding what their participation means (e.g., special development offerings, senior visibility, short-term assignments) and what it does not mean (e.g., guaranteed promotion).

Should High Potentials Be Told They Have Been Chosen?

Many employers in China do not want to formally declare someone as a high-potential employee. Instead, senior management prefers to keep those judgments and decisions confidential—even from the high potentials themselves. As a result, they risk losing these people to organizations that offer seemingly greater growth opportunities. In these situations, informing people of their high-potential status can serve as a retention aid. Good internal communication and transparency help to build trust and outweigh the downside.

Using Accelerated Development in China

Zijun Zhou, 30, has worked four years as the training and development manager of a container port company in southern China. She has a bachelor's degree from the United Kingdom and an MBA from a Canadian university earned via a distance-learning program. Prior to her current position, Zijun was the assistant dean in a small education institution. She joined the container company after deciding to embark on a business career.

Zijun is ambitious. In three to five years, she aims to be a competent HR director in a world-class, large or medium-sized enterprise. Her expectations are not unrealistic—her performance in her current position has been excellent, and she has just been selected for the company's Acceleration Pool.

Her boss, an expatriate manager, sees a great need to develop strong local HR talent. Bona fide HR professionals operating with truly Western standards are very rare in the China market.

Zijun's accelerated development commences with a vigorous assessment process to identify her strengths and areas for development. It includes one day at an Acceleration Center, where behavioral simulations are used to evaluate leadership and managerial skills. The Center provides Zijun with useful feedback on her strengths and development needs.

The assessment describes her as a good strategic thinker with good customer focus and excellent motivation. Her areas for development include developing others, influencing others, and establishing trusting relationships. Zijun's boss and her assigned mentor hold two meetings with her to design a structured development plan based on these results.

Zijun really appreciates the effort her boss and the company have put forth to aid her career development. She decides to tell her boss that even though she has been approached several times by headhunters, she now feels more committed than ever to her current employer.

The Payoff of Growing Your Own Leaders

Promotion decisions are by far the most sensitive staffing calls that organizations must make. Promotion criteria and decisions send a clear message about the types of workers and competencies valued by management. These decisions tend to be irreversible, especially in China. If someone fails to perform in the new job, then, for reasons of face, resignation is the only means of exit. So, making the wrong promotion decision becomes a disaster for the person, his or her manager, and the organization—more so in China than anywhere else.

Having a pool of people who have demonstrated technical, interpersonal, and management skills will make promotion decisions much easier and much more accurate. It's definitely worth the investment.

CHAPTER 12

Keeping Your Team

Finding good talent in China is hard; keeping it is even harder. That's why this entire chapter is devoted to retaining your team. The following six methods of keeping people longer have been suggested in previous chapters:

- Hire people who are motivated for the job, company, and location.
- Provide ongoing development opportunities at all levels.
- Develop a well-aligned, well-communicated performance management system and make sure everyone in your unit uses it.
- Help leaders create a more empowering environment.
- Promote local leaders who do a good job of developing and retaining their people.
- Have a functioning succession management system that identifies people with potential senior management talent and accelerates their development.

This chapter will reemphasize the importance of these strategies and present many new ideas, all aimed at increasing retention rates.

The Flight of Talent

Why do people leave? Is it a matter of money? Is the solution as simple as paying them more? A Corporate Leadership Council (CLC) survey found that, on average, professional employees in China earned an additional 22 percent when they switched jobs.[1] The global average was 16 percent. But once they change jobs, there's no guarantee that they will stay in that job either. Money is important, but it's only part of the story.

The 2007 Hewitt Associates' "Best Employer in Asia" survey, which ranked companies in China according to criteria such as employee satisfaction and training, found that the "best employers" did not necessarily pay the highest salaries.[2]

In 2007 DDI undertook a large survey on retaining staff in China. It yielded some interesting findings, including a widespread lack of commitment by Chinese workers toward their employers (when compared to other regions in the world). In fact, more than one-fifth (22 percent) of the Chinese employees surveyed said they were likely to leave their positions in the next year.[3] The mid- and executive-level leaders were the most likely to consider leaving. With high-level leaders much in demand in China, they are no doubt tempted by career opportunities elsewhere. The DDI survey also examined what drives people in China to leave a job for another. The 10 most common reasons they gave for switching employers are presented in Table 12.1.[4]

TABLE 12.1: Why Employees in China Leave Their Jobs

Reason For Leaving	%
1. Lack of growth/development opportunities	53%
2. Better career opportunity elsewhere	42%
3. Insufficient compensation	31%
4. Did not find the work interesting	22%
5. Insufficient rewards/recognition	21%
6. Insufficient benefits	21%
7. Did not feel efforts were appreciated	20%
8. Job was not what was expected	18%
9. Poor fit with the organizational culture	17%
10. External factors	17%

As Table 12.1 shows, compensation is important, but it is not the top-rated reason that employees leave a company. More critical to retention are the availability of employee growth and development offerings and the lure of better career opportunities in another organization.

Some companies actually design their China business model to account for expected employee retention problems. One of the world's largest software companies decided to establish several R&D centers in China. Its initial plan was to have teams work only on software testing. However, after the organization analyzed several business models and considered the overriding factor of employee retention, the plan shifted to include design, development, and test work, which would be more engaging. China would become an end-to-end provider for the company. Despite having one of the world's most recognized brands, the organization realized that testing alone was considered "second-class" work compared to design and development. Although this model cost more up front, it was necessary to provide a work environment that would offer interesting work, growth, and broader career opportunities, thereby promoting employee retention.

Of course, all companies take steps to retain their staff. But the DDI survey found that 79 percent of corporate HR respondents in China judged their retention efforts to be ineffective. And 99 percent said they needed to improve their retention efforts.[5] Many, however, were unsure of what to try next. The DDI results[6] offer suggestions for what an organization can do:

1. Improve selection, particularly focusing on job and organizational fit.
2. Provide leaders who value their people, foster an environment of trust, and show their appreciation.
3. Provide challenging growth opportunities in job responsibilities.

The importance of these three actions has been validated by DDI research throughout the world.

1. Improve Selection, Particularly Focusing on Job and Organizational Fit

"If you have only one dollar to spend on either improving the way you develop people or improving your selection and hiring process, pick the latter," said the late Douglas Bray, DDI's cofounder and renowned organizational psychologist. Of course, most organizations must divide their investment dollars between developing the people they already have and acquiring additional talent; nonetheless, the point still holds true. Assuming there is a sufficient supply of outside talent, an organization should place its highest priority on selecting the right people for jobs.

Particularly in China, young graduates often do not have a clear idea of what industry or profession they would like to be in. As a result, they choose an employer based on brand or reputation, hoping it will give them an advantage when they look for their next job. Expatriate managers are well advised to keep this in mind and not assume that every applicant really wants a career in their company or industry.

It is also important to hire the right people, because not everything can be taught. For example, training people to improve their judgment, learning agility, or adaptability is difficult, and perhaps impossible. Also, given the rapid growth that most businesses are experiencing in China, organizations lack enough time to develop people. It is cheaper and more efficient to hire people with good skills (if they are available), rather than to try to develop them later. Of course, this is why poaching is so prevalent in China. In short, you should never compromise on the quality of your hiring, even in China.

2. Provide Leaders Who Value Their People, Foster an Environment of Trust, and Show Their Appreciation

The DDI study of retention in China examined the relationship between satisfaction with 20 different work factors and employees' intentions to leave the organization within the next year. The factors most strongly related to intentions to stay were called retention drivers. The work characteristics in Table 12.2 are listed from most to least important as employee retention drivers. Those ranked in the top half of the list are considered primary retention drivers; the bottom half, secondary.

Two of the top three retention drivers are directly related to the quality of the employee's manager. That is, employees were most likely to want to stay with an organization if they had a good manager who recognized their contributions. By contrast, satisfaction with compensation was not a strong driver of retention, even though employees had cited it as one of the primary reasons for leaving their last position (see Table 12.1). Although organizations need to offer competitive salaries, compensation alone is insufficient for retaining valued talent. Rather, it is employees' dissatisfaction with various intangible aspects of work, particularly the organizations' leaders, that erodes their commitment and makes them vulnerable to outside offers.

TABLE 12.2: Why Employees Stay[7]

Work characteristics listed in rank order of importance to employees as retention drivers

Work Characteristics in Order of Importance	Employee Retention Drivers
A good manager/boss	Primary
Opportunity for accomplishment	Primary
Recognition for individual contributions	Primary
Great company leadership	Primary
A creative or fun workplace culture	Primary
A compatible work group/team	Primary
Opportunities to learn and grow	Primary
An organization you feel proud to work for	Primary
Interesting work	Primary
Opportunities for advancement	Primary
Benefits	Secondary
Employee autonomy (freedom to direct work)	Secondary
Balance between work and personal life	Secondary
Compensation	Secondary
Promise of stability/job security	Secondary
Employee lifestyle support	Secondary
Variety in the work	Secondary
Flexible work conditions	Secondary
Opportunity for expatriate assignments	Secondary
Amount of vacation/annual leave	Secondary

These data show how leadership is crucial for cutting turnover. Employees tend to leave their manager rather than their company. Workers who feel undervalued or disempowered are likely to leave even if they are well paid.

Having a good relationship with one's boss matters even more to employees in China than it does in the West. Here are eight things you can do as a manager to create a work environment that encourages people to stay:

- Act as a senior family member.
- Get to know your workers and their families.
- Conduct regular chats with the local employees.
- Be aware of your leadership impact.
- Make a special effort to show appreciation.
- Credit the team.
- Establish employee rewards and penalties.
- Communicate, communicate, communicate.

Act as a Senior Family Member

The paternalistic culture is deeply ingrained in every aspect of work and personal life. Today, managers in China can still expect to be invited to a wedding or special family celebration. During such events they might even be expected to give a speech or sit at the main family table. In your employees' eyes, this is an important role that you must assume. Your involvement and participation in their lives signal that they are a valued member of the work family. It gives them face, and it gives their parents and extended family face.

A Show of Respect

One manager and his pregnant wife were asked to the 100-day celebration of an employee's newborn son. As they entered the reception banquet, they were ushered into a special room with the main family in which, oddly, not a single person was smoking. This manager was then called up to the stage to say a few nice words about the couple and their baby. After dinner the manager and his wife got up to leave and, as they reached the door, what seemed like 50 people in the room lit cigarettes in unison. Everyone had refrained from smoking out of respect for the boss and his expectant wife.

It was important to the employee and his family that the boss came. In fact, the following day, the employee profusely thanked the manager for showing him and his parents such great respect. That person is still a loyal, committed employee eight years later.

Get to Know Your Workers and Their Families

In line with the leader-as-a-family-member role, another good retention idea is to connect with and leverage your workers' families. One multinational company in Shanghai organizes a "Family Day" and invites employees' family members to join this day of activities. Another event is "Get to Know Your Leader Day," during which managers can meet and get acquainted with their employees' family members. Out of respect, most Chinese employees also include their parents in such gatherings. Overall, the event provides an excellent opportunity for managers to demonstrate their interest in their employees and their families.

One Manager's Retention Plan

At a large company, one manager described how he has "saved" several retention-risk employees. At various times during the peak business season, he invites a valued employee and his or her spouse to dinner, during which he shows deep appreciation for the person as a core member of the organization. To the spouse he extends his thanks for his or her sacrifices during this period and goes on to explain various aspects of the company culture and values as well as what it is like to work in the organization. As a result of the dinner, the manager's employees on numerous occasions have expressed how their spouses became more engaged and supportive of their career in the company because the spouses felt personally more a part of it.

Conduct Regular Chats with the Local Employees

One senior expatriate manager connects with his local staff by holding regularly scheduled, one-on-one discussions over lunch. He also schedules 10 employees at a time for informal Friday gatherings. Discussions typically are balanced between work, personal matters, and career aspirations. In the process this manager has come to better know his staff members—from their thoughts on the business to their personal interests and motivations. This personal face time promotes a sense of family among the staff and provides him with valuable ideas and feedback.

A President's Simple Act Earns Respect

One multinational company's Asia president, based at a manufacturing site in Shanghai, wanted to show his attachment to the local team as well as his desire to learn from them. He made a point to always eat lunch in the factory canteen where all the workers ate. Most of the company's other expatriates ate there too, but they always sat in a group at one end of the canteen. The Asia president deliberately ate with the factory employees; rarely did he sit with the other expatriates. This simple act won him much respect and loyalty from his workers. It also gave them an opportunity to talk informally with him about the business.

Be Aware of Your Leadership Impact

Another practice that will earn the admiration of your Chinese team is to treat the local staff with respect in accordance with social norms. Saving and giving face are always important; this means not yelling at or even openly criticizing staff in front of colleagues. Chinese employees who feel that they are reprimanded unfairly or in a humiliating way—even in private—often will start to look for a different job. In addition, other employees likely will empathize with their reprimanded colleague, and morale will begin to deteriorate.

The Wrong Way to Make a Point

An expatriate manager from Europe was deployed by his software company as the service center vice president for Greater China. He was, in the view of headquarters, a high-potential manager who was expected to do well in his new assignment. But he had a tendency to lose his temper when things weren't going well. Sometimes he would even start screaming and continue doing so until the issue was resolved. Such outbursts might have been tolerated in his home country, but in China they have dire consequences.

The company had much valuable intellectual property on its employees' laptops and had instituted tight security measures. The manager had warned the employees on several occasions about one security measure in particular: Employees were to lock their laptops when they left the office.

One day when all the local staff had gone for lunch, the manager observed that not one laptop had been locked. So, he decided to make his point by taking everyone's machine and hiding them all in his office. As people returned from lunch, the manager sat in his office and watched as fright came over their faces. He waited about 30 minutes before calling everyone together to ask why they were so upset. No one responded. He then explained what he had done and why: He had wanted to demonstrate his point. To further emphasize his position, he then mocked some of the employees' reactions that he had witnessed to embarrass them.

Three employees resigned the following week.

Make a Special Effort to Show Appreciation

Saving and giving face are always important in China and essential for every leader. As a manager, you can provide positive reinforcement by:

- Acknowledging good performers within the organization. For example, in one organization, managers send departmental e-mail messages showing their appreciation for employees when they excel. This has caught on with employees, who now send e-mails sharing positive feedback among themselves.

- Complimenting employees on their good work—in private and in public. Don't limit your compliments to just your star performers; praise all your employees. An expatriate leader shared the story of one average, but solid, performer who walked into his office and talked of resigning. He immediately asked her why. She explained how bad it felt to hear everyone else in the office getting praise and recognition for their contributions while she was not. The lesson he learned was to make every effort to praise the big and small accomplishments of everyone—so that all feel valued.

- Appreciating your quiet workers as well as the extroverts. The quiet ones are waiting for your affirmation too; if they don't get it, they will eventually contribute to your staff turnover.

- Celebrating accomplishments frequently with staff lunches, Friday happy hours, and dinners at Chinese festivals. During these types of gatherings (either formal or informal), Chinese leaders typically take a moment to thank the team for their efforts. There is no reason that you, as an expatriate leader, should not do the same. This acknowledgment needs to be described with specific examples by you in a short speech rather than merely implied with the gesture of a lunch, dinner, etc. Chinese employees will then see the event as important for relationship building rather than simply as socializing at the company's expense.

- Recognizing individuals who make a special effort. Many Chinese employees will use their leisure time to undertake additional training and education—often at their own expense. They will find it reassuring that their efforts to better themselves are known and appreciated by the manager.

- Providing constructive, corrective feedback. Doing so will help you earn respect and show that you care about your staff. It is important, though, when giving the feedback to emphasize the positive aspects of an employee's performance rather than focusing on the negative. By providing constructive, balanced feedback, you get your point across without hurting the feelings of your Chinese employees.

A Valuable Employee Almost Lost

Donald, a senior software engineer, had worked for three years in a Taiwanese-owned software company in Shenzhen before submitting his resignation to his expatriate manager, a Hong Kong Chinese educated in Australia. Donald told his manager he was leaving to take care of family matters in northeastern China.

The manager was disappointed—Donald's departure would be a big loss to the team. During the farewell dinner, Donald's boss gave him a gift and a card in which he had jotted down his appreciation for Donald's efforts. Donald was taken aback. It was the first time in three years that his boss had ever acknowledged appreciation for his contributions. At the end of the dinner, Donald asked his boss if he might stay on in his old job after all.

His manager then realized the real reason that Donald wanted to leave: He did not feel valued, despite having recently received a big bonus. The boss understood that the bonus was not enough; instead, recognition needed to come from him personally and not just from "the company."

Chinese attach significant importance to personal relationships. In Donald's eyes, he only works for the company, but he has a real, one-on-one relationship with his manager.

Credit the Team

As an expatriate manager, there is a fundamental principle that will enable you to succeed in leading your local team: Understand that you are there to serve them. When your contract expires, you will leave, but your legacy will remain with the team you helped to build. Your results are not about you and your individual successes as an expatriate in China; instead, the credit must go to the whole team that is creating the results with you.

The Key to Success: Give Credit

At a Pan-Asia annual dinner, the company president was handing out several awards. The expatriate, who was a business unit general manager, won an award for a major project he had led. As the award was announced, he was surprised that all of his Chinese team members exploded with cheers. When called to the podium to make a speech, he began by saying that every project in Asia deserved to win. He then turned to the project team of 30 sitting in the audience and called them all up on stage, explaining that they were the real reason for this award. Once the team was on the stage, the manager handed over the microphone to the most senior team member to say a few words. Later, two senior leaders from two other countries in Asia explained to him why they thought he was successful in China: "You humbly give credit to your team, which gives face and wins the hearts of your employees."

Establish Employee Rewards and Penalties

Be clear on the agreed rewards and penalties, and be firm on their application. Chinese employees perceive fairness as one of the most basic rules of mutual trust. If you do not follow the rules and are not transparent, your Chinese employees won't be either. Nor will they respect you. Therefore, when your Chinese employees accomplish what they set out to do, recognize their achievements by granting higher-value responsibilities and special rewards. Likewise, if employees show patterns of failing to meet their commitments, be sure they know what the consequences will be and apply them. They might resign, but your actions will show others on the team that you have a low tolerance for mediocrity. Promotion via seniority is part of the "old" China; promotion by merit is what young, ambitious Chinese expect today.

Rewarding the Team: Incentive Trips

It's not uncommon to see magazine advertisements offering incentive trips for business teams. Here's an example of how these trips can be leveraged as a motivating reward.

Every year a multinational company's vice president holds a negotiation session with each office throughout his China operations. At the start of the fiscal year, he sets revenue targets for each branch. Halfway through the year, he allows the employees from each branch to commit to a higher revenue target. When a branch does so, he agrees that if the stretch target is met, a specified amount of money will be given for all branch members to travel to the team's chosen location. Over the years, as teams have hit their stretch goals, they have traveled to locations like Kunming, Sanya in China's Hainan Province, Italy, and Australia. And when teams failed to meet their stretch goals, they did not go anywhere, but no questions were asked and there were no complaints; people knew they did not reach their mark. Instead, this incentive produced only a greater drive in those failing branches to meet their numbers the next year.

Communicate, Communicate, Communicate

Hewitt Associates' *Best Employers* surveys show that if leaders and managers are more open, accessible, and willing to share key information, then employees will be far happier in their jobs.[8] Furthermore, when managers clearly communicate company strategies, goals, and targets to their staff, people are more likely to perform better and to identify with the organization. While this might seem obvious, 89 percent of the employees in organizations that Hewitt ranked as best employers said their company provided them with meaningful direction, compared with only 52 percent of the employees in the remaining companies.

Also, managers who engender high levels of trust pass along both good and bad news to their employees, including information about the company's finances, whatever their state. If managers refrain from hiding bad news from their local staff in China, they are more likely to earn people's respect and be seen as having high integrity.

The Power of Appreciation

According to Mark DeCocinis, vice president and area general manager of The Portman Ritz-Carlton, Shanghai, "We really are a family here at the hotel and we have a high level of trust among our people. Every morning we have a staff line-up, which not only provides a brief for the daily activities, it also reinforces our company values and reminds people that their efforts are both recognized and appreciated by the organization."[9] DeCocinis understands the basic principle that employees who feel undervalued are likely to leave even if they are well paid.

3. Provide Challenging Growth Opportunities in Job Responsibilities

As noted in earlier chapters, training and learning opportunities matter a great deal to Chinese professionals and managers, as do opportunities to show what they can accomplish at work. Development opportunities are a driver for both the attraction and retention of Chinese employees as well. Typically, Chinese employees are more concerned than their Western counterparts about career development, education, and training, and it is more than just development for development's sake—employees expect a job where they can apply what they have learned.

Getting New Employees Off to a Strong Start

An excellent way to build a strong, long-lasting relationship with a new employee is to deliver—on the person's first day—a clear message that you care about the individual's development and that you will support his or her efforts to be successful in the job. In China, this is particularly important given the preference for a strong leader–follower relationship.

But many managers spend little effort getting their employees off to a strong start, because they regard it as an HR responsibility with no real benefit. What follows are suggestions of various on-boarding practices in China that you can implement the day a new employee arrives:

On the First Day . . .

- Explain to the new hire how his or her job fits into the company as well as its relevance and importance. Often, individuals learn about aspects of their new job gradually. They are not given a holistic overview of what is to be accomplished and their specific role. Consequently, they fail to fully grasp the meaning of their work and how it supports broader company objectives.

- Discuss the job performance criteria that will be used in the organization's performance management system and explain how the system works. This way, the individual will know exactly what is expected of him or her and how this achievement will be evaluated.

- Share what you are looking for beyond the formal job requirements. For every job there are varied characteristics or job demands that go beyond the job description. Sometimes they are not written anywhere—they take the form of informal company rules and practices. But typically, new people don't learn them until they make a mistake.

- Review the results of the selection process, discussing how the person's identified strengths can be built upon in the new job and planning how his or her development needs (knowledge, job challenges, and competencies) can be addressed. This is a great way to start a solid relationship. The Success Profile^{SM} used in the selection process, as described in detail in Chapter 4, can become a road map for the individual's development while on the job. For example, knowledge and job challenge (experience) areas that the new employee lacks can be discussed, and development actions can be planned to enhance these areas. New hires generally are very impressed when you establish from day one the organization's commitment to their development.

- Plan how you will help the new hire make friends and attain mentors. Some new hires make quick contacts with their fellow workers and seek help about how things are done, expected procedures, and other such matters. They quickly develop internal mentors. But others are reluctant to be proactive in getting advice or help. There is a strong relationship between social networks, job success, and job satisfaction.

Ensure Career Development for Everyone

It is essential to focus on training and career development—not only for those high-potential employees in your Acceleration Pool®, but also for your entire staff. Your goal is to create a workplace environment in which everyone is being developed. Otherwise, employees who are not in the Acceleration Pool will become discouraged; they will feel like second-class employees and ultimately will leave. Although these employees might not be destined for top leadership positions, they still will be needed to fill mid-level positions in the leadership pipeline in a booming China economy.

Managers can provide career development opportunities by:
- Setting aside regular time to coach employees, who cherish face time with expatriate managers, because they see it as an opportunity to broaden their business acumen and international exposure.
- Providing stretch assignments in safe learning environments.
- Sponsoring overseas learning experiences or rotational learning roles.

- Adopting "hands-on" coaching for junior team members.
- Ensuring that junior staff get a range of tasks—not always the mundane ones.

Provide Learning Paths, if Not Career Paths

As noted in Chapter 3, visibility of a well-documented career structure is important to all Chinese employees. They want to know where their career is heading, the path they will be taking to get there, and what the job-level requirements and expectations are for each step. A career management system is seen in China as part of the paternalistic role that organizations and managers should play. Because of flat organization structures and frequent changes, it is often impossible for organizations to provide a real career path. Some substitute a learning path—what the individual will learn during the first three years. Companies also can leverage these learning paths to sell the value of lateral job movement as employees prepare themselves for the next level.

Conduct More Frequent Performance Reviews

In Chapter 10 we suggested that performance reviews should be held at least annually. But why not leverage them for retention purposes too? One way to do this is to conduct formal discussions quarterly regarding performance goals and their achievement. Your ambitious, results-driven Chinese employees are nearly always eager for more performance feedback. They want to be sure they are on track. At the same time, you benefit because such regular discussions provide an opportunity to manage their career expectations. Feedback from employees who have experienced frequent performance reviews reveals that they not only enjoy the face time with their boss, but they also are encouraged by their leader's efforts to help them grow.

Other Practical Considerations in Managing Retention

Following is a list of additional retention tactics that organizations and individuals are successfully implementing in China.

- As has been emphasized repeatedly, Chinese employees cherish their development. Some organizations use this fact to their advantage by offering formal, multiple-year training programs for new hires. One organization found that none of its newly hired, high-potential graduates left the company until after they completed the program. After analyzing the situation, the company decided to take two actions: extending the program from two to three years and directing the HR team to design an advanced program that extended the learning opportunities by another two years.   The organization speculates that if structured development is continuously offered, there will be less turnover.

- It is impossible to retain everyone in a labor market as mobile and buoyant as China's. New expatriate managers need to decide on whom they should concentrate their retention efforts. Initial retention efforts should focus on people who both provide significant value to the organization and are likely to leave.   Once the retention threats are identified, the next step is to determine their retention drivers. A quick-check retention discussion should be conducted. This will be the case particularly if a new expatriate manager has replaced another to whom existing Chinese staff felt close or loyal. They might feel less attached to the company because of that manager's departure.

  It also is essential to educate your head office to China's unique employee turnover and staffing situation.   You must customize your manpower planning model to the situation in China. If you don't, and you directly translate the head count or productivity plan from your head office to China, you are courting disaster. Your operations will end up too lean. Rather, you need to negotiate a grace period for your China operations before you can reach the company's global standards for head count or productivity levels.

- Status and image are given considerable weight in the Chinese culture. The value of a company being named a "Best Place to Work" or the boss being named as "Best Manager" cannot be overestimated as a way of building pride, recognition, and a sense of family.   When companies receive such honors, they proudly promote them. For example, in the front of SC Johnson's Shanghai building hangs an enormous banner stating the company's achievement as "Best Employer" (by Hewitt Associates). It serves as a great reminder to their employees each morning as they enter— and to prospective ones as they pass by. And it reminds all expatriate managers in China that the hiring game is one team sport in which they must excel. The retention game is another.

CHAPTER 13

Getting Off to a Fast Start

What determines whether you will have a good start in China? Much depends on how well you prepare and, once on the ground, how you establish yourself and adapt your leadership style to the unique challenges you'll face. This chapter is less of a "how to" guide and geared more toward the lessons learned from expatriates who have gone before. Learning from those who have real practical experience—those who have made their mistakes and grown from them—will provide an excellent road map for your getting off to a fast start in China. Although having such a road map can be helpful, you also must be ready to take detours and side trips to reach your own end destination. Make this journey yours with an educated awareness of what obstacles and barriers you might encounter.

Predeparture Preparation

The Transition Period

Once your China assignment is confirmed, no doubt you will feel eager to hit the ground running. But before your departure, you must prepare yourself to completely disconnect from your current job by completing any unfinished projects and offloading your main work responsibilities.

If you do retain certain responsibilities, be clear with your organization about what you will be held accountable for and what will be offloaded. One major distraction facing many expatriates during their first few months in China is the constant pull of their past job and former responsibilities.

The first step in preparing for your departure is to list your current main areas of responsibility and the proportion of your time associated with those activities. Then list your responsibilities for your future role in China. Comparing the two lists provides a picture of what will need to be transitioned before your departure.

Once you have done this analysis, ensure a clean break by:

- Identifying those individuals who will take over your former role and responsibilities.
- Documenting and communicating a transition plan of who is responsible for what and starting when.
- Understanding what training, coaching, and guidance will be required from you and others to provide the skills necessary for a successful transition. Share, as necessary, your subject matter expertise and relevant organizational knowledge. Set others up for success before your departure, as your time will be consumed once you are on the ground in China.
- Making necessary introductions and transition meetings with customers and external partners so that they understand that your responsibilities have been officially handed over.
- Ensuring that your transition plan is well documented and formally communicated to key partners in the organization. This informs them of who becomes accountable for which aspects of your former role.

Taking these critical steps will enable a proper transition from your old role to your new assignment. By removing the distractions that can commonly occur in a job transition, you gain more focus for your new challenges and tasks during your China assignment's first few months.

Networking

Soon the reality sets in that you will be leaving friends and family for a mysterious country and culture. In addition, you will be leaving those business contacts and networks—both in and out of your company—that have supported your success to date. Now it is important to build up networks that can support your success in China. There are three simple steps to building a supportive network:

1. Connect with senior leadership on strategies, plans, and advice.
2. Strengthen your internal relationships.
3. Establish contact with external customers and partners.

1. Connect with senior leadership on strategies, plans, and advice.

Before leaving, make appointments with senior leaders who have interests in the China market (most do). Explain your intended focus and strategies for achieving your assignment's goals and objectives, and then check for their agreement and ideas. Even if their business is not directly affected by your assignment, it is still advisable to make as many internal connections as you can, because you certainly will be serving as a conduit of information between the home office and the China operation. Beyond sharing your goals and plans, take the opportunity to ask questions and gain their perspectives on China. For example, how will the China operation affect the company's future business? Is China in their short- or long-term strategy? What contacts do they have in China? What advice do they have?

2. Strengthen your internal relationships.

The second step is to strengthen your current internal networks and relationships before leaving. These will help you quickly navigate your organization from afar. The people you are connected with can provide you and your team with just-in-time information and keep you abreast of the organization, its changes, new directions, and so on. And your professional networks will help you obtain those elusive or complex answers that you need to support your China business. When well leveraged, your networks and relationships help you identify the right people to get things done.

This is where your Chinese associates, regardless of their fluency in your organization's native language, will look to you for help. Networks in your home country as well as global ones can bring you quick, easy wins in the eyes of your local team. One important caution: Do not allow the local team to become overly reliant on you for communications outside of China. One expatriate in a German company made a point to identify the right people in Düsseldorf for his China staff to contact, introduced the local team, and encouraged the two parties to communicate directly. Not only did both sides benefit, but both the local team and the associates outside China developed important internal contacts.

3. Establish contact with external customers and partners.

The third networking step relates mostly to people outside your organization. Make an effort to arrange meetings with clients who have operations or interests in China. Use these sessions to gain a better understanding of your new market. Another objective for these interactions is to start setting up post-arrival meetings with your client contacts based in China. These will serve as entry points into the market as well as social networks.

Cultural Considerations

One expatriate has shared that when he started to tell colleagues and friends about his upcoming assignment in China, they would typically ask three questions:

- "Are you learning the language?"
- "Are you reading books on Chinese culture?"
- "How crazy are you?"

What follows is a compilation of cultural lessons learned based on expatriate reflections of what worked, what didn't, and what they would have done differently during their preparation phase.

Language

Most expatriates highly recommend learning some Mandarin. This need not mean to the extent of business-level fluency; general conversation or survival proficiency will be enough. Your actions to embrace the language will be perceived as a sign of respect and appreciation for Chinese culture. One non-Chinese-speaking expatriate revealed how guilty he was made to feel by customers and colleagues when asked if he could speak Chinese. He felt that the locals continued to show genuine disappointment in his language shortcomings. By making the effort to learn the language, you will garner much respect in the office and from external partners and customers.

Learning the language will not only help you manage your day-to-day personal situations and work with your staff, but also facilitate your understanding of the behaviors and culture you will encounter. However, while speaking the language can be an ice-breaker or relationship-builder in informal settings, you should always work through a trusted interpreter in formal meetings—both within and outside your company. In these settings you should never speak the language, no matter how well you know it, if for no other reason than to be able to blame a serious disagreement or conflict on the misinterpretation, rather than deal a fatal blow to the business relationship. Both you and the Chinese will appreciate and respect this style; it will allow both sides to save face in any formal communication, a concept that is inherently Chinese. By working through an interpreter, you set the stage for both sides to have a successful meeting.

China Culture/Business Books and Training

There is an abundance of books and articles about the do's and don'ts in China. Many expatriates have fond memories of scouring through these volumes with the reverence that might be reserved for a religious text. Also, there are services that provide business- and family-related culture classes, all of which are helpful as a foundation to build a better understanding of what you are about to encounter. But most expatriates soon realize that, although it is helpful to understand the basic do's and don'ts, this book knowledge will be quickly challenged in the real China. While books should entail a significant part of your preparation, they should not be the sole source for it. What you learn in books should advise you, but not drive you. Always keep in mind that your pre-posting education is only meant to help you get off on the right foot; once you have landed, your openness to new experiences and people will enable your China tour to become one of your life's greatest learnings. One Chinese business leader put it another way: Although these books mention that Chinese people are very different from each other, some expatriates may develop stereotyped perspectives from the general remarks described in them. So, it is strongly suggested that you stay open to the people you interact with in China and keep exploring by yourself, instead of simply being guided by books you have read about China.

A Bridge Between Home and the Chinese Culture

Before moving to China, meet with expatriates who have recently returned from a tour there. You will be surprised by how many there are; they can be found with a little social networking. Also, meet with Chinese people living in your hometown. Depending on how long it has been since they left China, they can be a great source of information. This group should be able to provide insight on the experience of working and living in the Chinese culture and specific key differences between your home and Chinese cultures. For example, the reality of working as a German leader within a Chinese cultural setting is completely different from an Australian's experience. Similarly, Americans will have different experiences, as will Singaporeans.

Culture Fit Visit

Consider a "cultural exploration visit." Regardless of when it occurs in your predeparture preparations, a visit is a way to explore and test your initial perceptions of the Chinese culture as well as the China organization you will be joining. Here are several expatriate suggestions to consider when planning your visit:

- **Local staff**—Meet and spend time talking with the local staff. Your objective is to learn about them, the business, the market, and what motivates them. This meet-and-greet must be done with the highest sensitivity. Not only are you there to have a taste of what's to come, but also your colleagues want to learn about you, your experience, and your plans. It is important that you do not come across as a corporate interrogator—this is a diplomatic first meeting and begins the foundation for building trust. It is important that you come across as humble and prepared to listen.

- **Customers and partners**—Don't limit your meetings to associates; talking with customers and partners will help to build your understanding of the China market. Encounters with the market will help to shape and refine your strategies and plans. In addition, you can identify the low-hanging fruit (i.e., opportunities) that will help you make an immediate impact and score quick wins.

- **Expatriates**—Talk with other expatriates from your country who are living and working in China. They are your information source to get the scoop on the business realities facing the *laowai* (i.e., the foreigner). Ask how their initial expectations of their expatriate assignment differed from their current understanding of doing business in China. Meeting this group also will help you establish a fast-start network into the local expatriate business community.

- **Go local**—Another aspect of this trip should be to live among the locals, rather than staying at a high-end hotel in the tourist part of town. Many cities in China offer apartments that are located in areas where you can walk and interact with the culture. By engaging in the local environment, you gain glimpses into how people live, what matters to them, how they interact with one another, how they sell, how they negotiate, their views on the world and China's place in it, and so on. This type of experience also provides credibility when talking with locals in your office—you can share, among other stories, how you "survived the subway during rush hour."

An Asian leader shared his observation of Western expatriates on their "cultural visits," breaking it down into two types of people. One group stays in upscale hotels in central tourist districts. Typically during their visit, they look for villas in expatriate compounds, investigate schools, and have a company driver escort them at all times. This group refrains from immersing themselves in the culture. The other group typically explores the city, takes public transportation, shops at local food stores, and tries local restaurants with new colleagues. Basically, this group uses their visit to truly experience China. In this leader's opinion, the latter group excels more in connecting with their team, building local networks and relationships, and minimizing culture shock. Overall, their ramp-up time is much shorter.

China Is China

Understand that China is not Asia and vice versa. It would be a horrible mistake to homogenize Asian countries. Although the majority of Singaporeans are of Chinese origin and their culture has a powerful Chinese influence, they are not like the mainland Chinese. Most Singaporeans have just as difficult a time adjusting to China as do Westerners. The education system, business market maturity, country size, British colonialism, and numerous other unique Singaporean factors have shaped the way that country has formed its business culture. Hong Kong Chinese who were brought up in British colonialism also act and think differently from the mainland Chinese. The Taiwanese Chinese perceive themselves as drastically different from mainland Chinese because of their ideological and political differences.

One of the biggest faux pas that some expatriates make is to think China and Japan are the same. The reality is that the relationship between these two countries is extremely sensitive. One expatriate shared the story of taking a senior executive who had done work in Japan to meet a key prospect in Northern China. The expatriate noticed some slight indifference from the Chinese prospect when the senior executive introduced himself and explained his extensive work with the Japanese. That indifference turned into annoyance when the senior executive made several comments stereotyping similarities between the Chinese and Japanese. That was an enormous mistake. After the meeting, the once-eager Chinese prospect was slow to respond to the expatriate's calls and inquiries. When they finally connected, the message delivered was "your senior manager does not know us and does not know our business," and the prospect offered no opportunities for cooperation. There are still many sensitivities about Japan that relate to World War II. If anything, these sensitivities have intensified in recent years, rather than diminished over time.

Culture Shock

Culture shock is real—it is a genuine psychological condition that can be extremely stressful for individuals who are placed into a different cultural environment. Culture shock usually starts its cycle within the first weeks of moving to a new environment, although sometimes it can take longer to surface. In 1954 anthropologist Kalvero Oberg described these five distinct stages of culture shock:[1]

- **Honeymoon Phase**—During the first few days, a newcomer experiences excitement in seeing new sights, meeting new people, and sampling the new culture.

- **Rejection Phase**—The newcomer soon begins to experience problems adjusting to the rigors of a new routine and an unfamiliar environment and culture. The person might even begin to feel unwelcome and start resenting his or her new country.

- **Regression Phase**—The individual starts to wistfully recall and rely on the past—speaking in his or her home language; craving entertainment, news, and food from home; and seeking out others from home or those who speak the home language. The person might spend time complaining about the local customs and culture.

- **Recovery Phase**—The person eventually becomes comfortable with his or her new country, its language and customs, and its ways of doing things. The individual has completely adjusted to the change and has accepted the host country's way of life.

- **Return Culture Shock Phase**—When the person returns home, comfortable in the ways of the former host country, he or she must readjust to the culture of the home country. Changes may have occurred at home, and it might take some time for the newly repatriated individual to become at ease.

It is important to understand the stages of culture shock and how they can affect your business judgment and behavior. The hindsight advice from expatriates is to be aware of these stages so that you can manage your actions to limit their negative influence.

One expatriate marked his calendar with the approximate time he expected to spend in each stage. He outlined the symptoms and feelings he anticipated he would experience during each stage, and then formulated specific personal actions he would take to deal with them. He thought through these actions in advance of his posting so that he would not get lost in his feelings. For example, one behavioral symptom he was concerned about was the increased avoidance of local contact during the Rejection Phase. So, his planned action during that stage was to schedule weekly, informal lunches with his local team.

Self-Assessment

When considering your expatriate posting in China, the reality sets in on what you need to accomplish there. But then you realize that there are even more fundamental questions, such as:

- "How should I get things accomplished?"
- "How do I break through the China market?"
- "What will really be different?"
- "How should I adapt my own behaviors as a leader of a Chinese team?"

In order to put this book's learning into practice, you need an understanding of your current leadership strengths and gaps. One approach is to conduct a quick self-assessment of the core expatriate leadership competencies and any other competencies critical to your specific assignment. The purpose of this self-assessment is to provide you with insight into those behaviors demanding special attention. After the self-assessment, note how you will develop the needed behaviors before your departure as well as how you will proactively manage them once posted in your assignment. Table 13.1 highlights core behaviors that DDI has identified as being essential to expatriate leadership success. Use the column at the right to rate each competency as a strength, proficiency, or development area.

It is very important to understand that the behaviors that helped you achieve your current success might actually be derailers in the Chinese environment. For example, your innate tendency to be results oriented might have earned you the China posting, and although delivering results will be essential in your new role, how you get them will require different approaches, skills, and behaviors in Shanghai, Chengdu, or Beijing compared with those used in New York, London, or Frankfurt.

TABLE 13.1: Core Competencies for Expatriate Leaders

Competencies	Evaluate Your Ability as a Strength, Proficiency, or Development Area
Cultural Interpersonal Effectiveness—Demonstrating an understanding of and effective adaptation to varying interpersonal styles and norms across cultures; taking actions to minimize the stresses of cross-cultural experiences and using them as opportunities for growth.	
Developing Strategic Relationships—Using appropriate interpersonal styles and communication methods to influence and build effective relationships with business partners (e.g., peers, functional partners, external vendors, and alliance partners).	
Coaching/Teaching—Providing timely coaching, guidance, and feedback to help others excel on the job and meet key accountabilities.	
Empowerment/Delegation—Using appropriate delegation to create a sense of ownership of higher-level organizational issues and encouraging individuals to stretch beyond their current capabilities.	
Team Development—Using appropriate methods and interpersonal styles to develop, motivate, and guide a team toward successful outcomes and attainment of business objectives.	
Driving Execution—Translating strategy into operational reality; breaking down strategies or business initiatives into key tasks and identifying accountabilities; aligning communication, people, culture, processes, resources, and systems to ensure effective implementation and delivery of required results.	
Energy—Demonstrating the physical and mental stamina necessary to meet the challenges of organizational demands.	
Executive Disposition—Conveying an image that is consistent with the organization's values; demonstrating the qualities, traits, and demeanor (excluding intelligence, competence, or special talents) that command leadership respect.	

Arrival Adaptability

Chinese Names[2]

How the Chinese name themselves will be one of the first complexities that you will face upon arrival in China. Although there are perhaps 6,000 possible Chinese surnames, many have died out; today, there are approximately 3,100 surnames in active use. Almost a third of the population, or 350 million people, share one of just five surnames: pronounced in Mandarin as Zhang, Wang, Li, Zhao, and Chen. However, each is pronounced differently in the southern Chinese dialects—the ancestral dialects of most Chinese who live outside China. For example, *Zhang* is pronounced as "Chong" in Hakka, "Chang" in Hokkien, "Cheung" in Cantonese, and "Teo" in Teochew. *Wong,* the most popular surname in Hong Kong, is pronounced as "Wang" in Mandarin, "Heng" in Teochew, and "Ong" in Hokkien.[3]

Some mainland Chinese adopt more Western-sounding names based on their Chinese names. For example, An Na might choose to Westernize her name as Anna An, and Pan Yi might become Penny Pan. Others simply do a straight translation of their given names from Chinese to English, which is fine except that in some cases, names that are unremarkable in Chinese seem odd in English. For example Li Haijun might Westernize his name as Navy Li because Haijun means "Navy" in Chinese. In English, Zuo You is rendered as "Left Right." Others have names that reflect the Communist era. Chen Da Hong is one example—Chen is a common family name, but Da Hong means "Big Red" or "Really Red." Hopefully, this explanation will help reduce the surprise factor when you encounter an unusual name for the first time, such as Veggie, Cocaine, Sunflower, or Happy.

Another interesting trend for mainland Chinese is to adopt Western-sounding names according to their company's country of origin. It's not uncommon to find local Chinese staff in the Beijing office of an American multinational who call themselves John, Paul, or Rachel. Go to the office of a French multinational and you'll likely find yourself dealing with local Chinese who've adopted names such as Marcel, Francois, and Michele.

Establish Yourself and Your Position

The first question asked of most expatriates when they arrive in China—by both internal associates and customers—is, "How long will you be here?" This is not polite small talk. The locals are trying to determine the energy they should put into developing a relationship with you. If you say you have a two-year contract, then the locals immediately begin a countdown to the day you will be gone.

While there is no reason to announce the duration of your China assignment, don't think for a moment that your Chinese staff won't be aware of how long you will be in the country. Certain telltale signs, such as a fixed-term housing lease, quickly will become common knowledge to your staff. The best approach to questions regarding your term is to downplay the time aspect of your assignment and instead emphasize the goals and objectives you have set for your China operation.

When a local partner asked one expatriate during her first month when she was leaving, she effectively sidestepped the issue by clearly stating her business focus in China without mentioning any time frames, sharing how much she and her family loved living and working in China, and saying that she would like to stay as long as they let her.

Also, your staff will want to know how you fit into the organization and how they should relate to you in your role. Titles are not necessarily transparent; people will want to know how your authority is derived, how you are connected, and who you know. This is one reason that business cards are studied so intently when they are exchanged.

During your first month it is critical to establish yourself in the office as well as in the external market. Prepare a well-versed "elevator" speech (i.e., a brief explanation that you could recite in the time it takes you to ride the elevator to your office's floor) describing your position title (remember your title means a lot to locals, so pay special attention to it), responsibilities, education, and past professional experience. Both internals and externals will use this initial communication from you to sort out your status in the pecking order.

Set Direction for Your China Team

In Chinese employees' perception and standards of measurement, the leader's first test (for Chinese and expatriates alike) is to set direction. It is very important to pass this test. If you fail, your credibility will dissipate, and you will be unable to properly install the remaining building blocks (e.g., sales forecasts, budgets, operating plans) no matter how hard you work on them.

You must be able to articulate a clear vision and goals regarding what you want to accomplish in China. Doing so will help you gain the trust and respect of your senior local staff, who, being native to the China environment, will help you sculpt action plans to implement a strategy that will work in China.

Your Accountabilities and Alignment with Headquarters

With your headquarters manager and other staff, be clear on what you are being held accountable for during your assignment. Most expatriate assignments are linked to the company's overarching strategy and merit executive-level attention.

If there is any confusion about your role between the corporate objectives and those of the local management team, then it is critical to align all parties. For some expatriates, this is the toughest line to balance—between the home office's wants and the local office's needs.

Probably 8 of 10 expatriates will tell you that their job today has a different focus compared to their initial understanding. Why do so many expatriate assignments change? Expatriates explain that once they arrive and gain a better understanding of their business landscape, the operational realities in China influence shifts in their role's direction. (Chapter 6 examines the need for speed in developing a strategy for your area of responsibility.)

Who Are the Influential Local Leaders?

Locate those individuals who have the respect and trust of the local team. This does not mean those senior leaders who are revered, but rather, those formal or informal leaders within the organization whom associates look to for advice, guidance, and direction. Their strong following might be due to their relatively long tenure, age, or technical expertise within the organization. Quickly identify these individuals and the extent that they influence others. Learn their motivations and leverage them early on as you attempt to understand business opportunities as well as how to sway others' thinking and actions.

Understanding the Operational Realities

You will need to assemble the puzzle about the operational realities of your business. No matter how much you read about China or investigate the local operations, you will get only a surface understanding of the business. Upon your arrival, many of the local employees will respond cautiously to your presence. Most will share only what they feel you need to know or what serves their own needs. You will recognize huge gaps in their information, so ask detailed follow-up questions to uncover true meanings. You might find yourself asking several, so be careful not to turn your discussions into inquisitions.

Certainly, you cannot expect to learn everything about the business realities of your work environment during the first few months. Regardless of the questions you ask, you will rarely expose the real situation or root causes of day-to-day events in a straightforward manner. As trust builds, you will start to hear more and more about these. You will be amazed at how much more you will know compared to your initial understandings. Your acquisition of knowledge about the business should become a continuous activity in order to make sound business decisions and take decisive action. Uncovering all that you need to know requires patience; carefully selecting the right questions for the right people will enable you to piece together the information to complete the puzzle.

Keep in mind that your role as an expatriate is *not* to be Chinese. You do not look, act, or speak like a local Chinese (no matter how fluent you are). There are certain things that can be accomplished only between locals, just as there are certain things that only the expatriate can accomplish.

Patience + Place = Long-Term Respect

Some expatriates find it challenging to interact with the management team and even local senior leadership once they are in China. One expatriate who had been well engaged with the company's global strategy and decisions found that in China his daily work was distant from the overall corporate strategy. Adding to his frustration was the lack of a local transparent strategy and execution plan. Although the China operation was meeting its revenue targets, there remained a lack of communication regarding its long-term direction. When he asked the local senior management team questions about the strategy and direction, as he did back in the head office, he was surprised by the absence of any substance in the reply. As time went on, he realized there was, indeed, a strategy in place; maybe it wasn't sophisticated, but it was a strategy and plan nonetheless. His patience and well-positioned suggestions on strategy and direction started to pay off by getting him closer to the senior management team's thinking. His initiation was complete when a senior manager used his ideas to position the country-level strategy for a group of corporate executives. From that day forward, he was connected with the local senior management team's thinking and how it perceived the China operation. Several years later the country manager mentioned to the expatriate how concerned the management team had been that he was a head office spy, so they purposefully chose what and what not to share. However, the country manager went on to say that the expatriate earned his membership by practicing patience, sharing his ideas (rather than pushing them), and acting as a member of the local team.

The lesson here is to have patience. Nothing will get done when you expect it, nor will the results be what you expected—at least at first. And people will not pursue their objectives in the manner you would expect or perhaps even in a manner that makes sense to you. You have to understand this up front and decide early on what is really important and what is not. Keep your communications simple, remaining aware that your words may convey a variety of meanings to your Chinese staff. For example, the word "may" can mean either "shall" or "might." The word "finally" can be an expression of frustration or can denote something that is done for the last time.

On the Job 24/7/365

The excitement of your new China assignment's challenges and rewards will drive you hard to achieve the desired results. Work can easily become engaging to the point that it becomes all-consuming. Your role likely will necessitate navigating ambiguity, participating in late-night and early-morning conference calls, dealing with e-mails around the clock, maintaining old networks, nurturing new local relationships during late-night entertaining, and, if you have family in China, balancing family matters. Added to your workload is the fact that your mind will be bombarded by new cultural experiences and an unfamiliar language. This environment can easily become overwhelming and exhausting.

When does the expatriate get a chance to rest and recharge? It is not easy. Your usual national and religious holidays (such as Boxing Day, Independence Day, and Christmas) are not observed locally, and the Chinese national holidays are rarely known by your corporate partners. All of which means it is an extreme test for expatriates to disconnect and recharge. As one expatriate put it, he was constantly "on," whether working in the office, closing an important deal on a revered holiday, or just stopping at the vegetable market. Be mindful of how all these factors can wear on you personally as well as on your productivity. The main advice given from seasoned expatriates is to proactively manage and plan your quality of life. Without appropriate attention to this factor, burnout and work inefficiencies will slowly take over. And if you have young children in China, be sure to take time out for them; they will only be young once, and they will be dealing with their own cultural adjustments.

Stay Connected

During your first three months in China, you will be operating in overdrive. Most likely, you will be consumed with everything you need to accomplish locally. However, it is important to remember your networks back home too. Send back periodic updates so others don't think you have forgotten about them and so they don't forget about you. An American expatriate told how his senior leaders and colleagues enjoyed hearing about his personal and work experiences. His colleagues often offered advice, condolences, and encouragement, and shared humorous anecdotes about their involvement in similar experiences. Sharing his experiences with people who understood him and his culture was not only enjoyable, but also provided a platform for him to reconnect into his home culture.

Another way expatriates can stay connected is through a formal or informal role as a communication conduit. This sensitive task will require your best diplomatic skills as you maintain networks and relationships both locally and afar. Using your best judgment and internal political sensitivity, you can share insights on your growing analysis of the market, the operational realities, and local talent.

It is almost a guarantee that during your time in China you will leverage your networks back home for support of one kind or another. Take note of those people who have helped you be successful. Then, when visiting during your home leave, follow the traditions of your Asian counterparts and arrive bearing local gifts for them. Remember, it will be these networks that will support your repatriation when it is time to go home once your exciting expatriate assignment has ended.

It Has Been Our Pleasure

We hope this book has been helpful to you. It certainly has been great fun sharing our experiences and insights. In the course of writing *Leadership in China: An Expatriate's Guide,* we have learned a lot ourselves, reinforcing our view that one can never fully understand the fascinating country that is China.

If you have questions or wish to discuss any issues pertaining to this book, you can reach the authors through any of DDI's 76 offices around the world.

For more information about DDI, visit our web site at www.ddiworld.com.

END NOTES

Introduction

1. From "More Than Half of Chinese Can Speak Mandarin," from Xinhua News Agency's *China View,* March 7, 2007. Available online at: http://news.xinhuanet.com/english/2007-03/07/content_5812838.htm

2. From *CEO Challenge 2007: Top 10 Challenges* (pp. 10–11), by The Conference Board, 2007, New York: Author.

3. From "China's Looming Talent Shortage," by Diana Farrell and Andrew J. Grant, 2005, *The McKinsey Quarterly,* (4), pp. 70–79.

4. The Chinese statistic is from "Growing Today's Chinese Leaders for Tomorrow's Needs: Developing Business Leaders Could Make or Break China's Economic Growth," by Ronnie Tan and Richard Wellins, November 2006, "India & China Inc." supplement to *T+D, 60,* p. 21. Available through DDI's web site at: http://www.ddiworld.com/pdf/td_novci_supplement.pdf

    The global statistic is from *Leadership Forecast 2005–2006* (pp. 28–29), by Paul R. Bernthal and Richard S. Wellins, 2005, Pittsburgh, PA: Development Dimensions International.

Chapter 1

1. From *Asia Future Shock: Business Crisis and Opportunity in the Coming Years* (chapter 10), by Michael Backman, 2007, New York: Palgrave Macmillan.

2. From "Chaos in the Classrooms," a 2006 article that appeared in *The Economist, 380,* pp. 32–33. Available online at: http://www.economist.com/world/asia/displaystory.cfm?story_id=7279166

3. Estimated 2007 statistics are from the Chinese version of the Ministry of Education of the People's Republic of China web site (www.moe.gov.cn), on the page "Number of Students in Regular HEIS by Field of Study" (http://www.moe.edu.cn/edoas/website18/info33545.htm). The estimates are as follows: Anticipated number of 2007 graduates: 4,587,743. Of these, 1,355 will have a degree in philosophy; 244,609, in economics; 206,576, in law; 347,380, in education; 655,382, in literature; and 12,611, in history. In all, 1,467,913 (i.e., 32 percent) of the total 2007 graduates will have earned a humanities-related degree; of these, 281,262 students took these studies in a foreign language.

4. From *Asia Future Shock,* Backman, p. 72.

5. From "China Strives for World-Class Universities," by Howard W. French, October 28, 2005, *International Herald Tribune,* section 3, p. 2.

6. From "India's Skill Shortage," by Salil Tripathi, January 5, 2006, *The Wall Street Journal Asia,* p. 13.

7. From *Asia Future Shock,* Backman, p. 73.

8. From "China's Looming Talent Shortage," by Diana Farrell and Andrew J. Grant, 2005, *The McKinsey Quarterly,* (4), pp. 70–79.

9. From *Leadership in China: Keeping Pace with a Growing Economy* (pp. 5–7), by Paul R. Bernthal, Jason Bondra, and Wei Wang, 2005, Pittsburgh, PA: Development Dimensions International. Available through DDI's web site at: http://www.ddiworld.com/pdf/ddi_leadershipinchina_rr.pdf

10. From *Big in Asia: 30 Strategies for Business Success* (p. 200), by Michael Backman and Charlotte Butler, 2007, New York: Palgrave Macmillan.

11. Ibid.

12. From "China MBAs: Most Likely to Fall Short," by Dexter Roberts, 2006, *Business Week,* (4012), pp. 106–107. Available online at: http://www.businessweek.com/magazine/content/06_49/b4012094.htm

13. From "China's Counterfeit Culture Is Quite an Education," by Michael Backman, March 28, 2007, *The Age.* Available online at: http://www.theage. com.au/news/business/chinas-counterfeit-culture-is-quite-an-education/2007/03/27/1174761469475.html

14. From "China Suffers from Worst Brain Drain in the World," by Peter Harmsen, February 13, 2007, *Agence France-Presse.* Available online at: http://www.industryweek.com/ReadArticle.aspx?ArticleID=13604

15. From "U.S. Companies Facing Skills Shortage," by Yin Ping, November 2, 2006, *China Daily.* Available online at: http://en.bcnq.com/bizchina/2006-11/02/content_722530.htm

16. From "China's People Problem," a 2005 article that appeared in *The Economist, 375,* pp. 53–54.

17. From "Narrowing China's Corporate Leadership Gap," by Andrew Grant and Georges Desvaux, May 18, 2005, *China Daily.* Available online at: http://www.chinadaily.com.cn/english/doc/2005-05/18/content_443284.htm

18. From "China's Talent Wars," by Benjamin Robertson, March 2007, *Workforce Management Online.* Available online at: http://www.workforce. com/section/06/feature/24/78/95/index.html

19. From "Job Hopping Is Rampant as China's Economy Chases Skilled Workers," by Don Lee, February 21, 2006, *Los Angeles Times,* p. C-1.

20. From "2007 Beijing City Compensation and Benefits Study Result Presentation," by Hewitt Consulting, September 17, 2007, Beijing City, China, using *2007 Hewitt China TCM Study Beijing Findings.*

21. Ibid.

22. Ibid.

23. From "Salary Growth: What You Earn," a short article and graphic that appeared in *The Economist,* March 29, 2007. Available online at: http://www.economist.com/daily/chartgallery/displaystory.cfm?story_id=8909327

24. From "China's New Weapon: Low Executive Pay," by Michael Kanellos, June 4, 2007, *ZDNET News*. Available online at: http://news.zdnet.com/2100-9595_22-6188306.html

25. From "China's Pay Problems," posted by Ed Frauenheim, March 14, 2007, to *Workforce.com*. Available online at: http://www.workforce.com/wpmu/globalwork/2007/03/14/china%E2%80%99s-pay-problems/

26. From "A China Bank Chief Lags Behind in Pay," a section of the Shakers column "ABB Planning to Use Cash for Acquisitions" featured in the *International Herald Tribune,* May 11, 2006. Available online at: http://www.iht.com/articles/2006/05/10/bloomberg/bxshake.php

27. From "China's Contract Law: Something for Everyone," by Ed Frauenheim, August 20, 2007, *Workforce Management, 86,* pp. 35–39. The text of the Law of the People's Republic of China on Employment Contracts available online at: http://www.ckc.mofcom.gov.cn/ciweb/kcc/info/Article.jsp?a_no=96609&col_no=745

28. From "Hewitt Announces Best Employers in China 2007," a Hewitt Associates press release, April 20, 2007. Available online at: http://www.hewittassociates.com/Intl/AP/en-CN/AboutHewitt/Newsroom/PressReleases/2007/april-18-2007_a.aspx

Chapter 2

1. From *Big in Asia: 30 Strategies for Business Success,* by Michael Backman and Charlotte Butler, 2007, New York: Palgrave Macmillan.

2. From "A Critical Eye on Shanghai: Will the City's Extraordinary Growth Continue?" by Iain McDaniels, January 2004, *China Business Review*. Available online at: http://www.chinabusinessreview.com/public/0401/shanghai_letter.html

3. Adapted by DDI from the U.S. Census Bureau's International Data Base. Population pyramid available online at: http://www.census.gov/cgi-bin/ipc/idbpyry.pl?cty=CH&maxp=67043344&maxa=100&ymax=300&yr=2007&.submit=Submit+Query

4. From *China Global Comparison—Leadership Forecast 2005–2006* (pp. 8–11), by Paul R. Bernthal and Richard S. Wellins, 2005, Pittsburgh, PA: Development Dimensions International. Available through DDI's web site at: http://www.ddiworld.com/pdf/ddi_leadershipforecast2005_report_cn.pdf

The comparison survey respondents ranged in age from 18 to 55, but only a small percentage was over 45 (5 percent); thus, the findings contained within it are a good reflection on the young workers in China. The age breakdown for the *China Global Comparison* was as follows: less than 18 years, 0%; 18–25, 2%; 26–35, 51%; 36–45, 41%; 46–55, 5%; 56–65, 0%; and more than 65, 0%.

5. From "China's Next Generation: Perspectives on Future Leaders," a speech given by John L. Thornton, professor and director of global leadership at Tsinghua University (Beijing), at the S.C. Fan Memorial Lecture held at The University of Hong Kong, March 15, 2006.

6. From "A Thousand Chinese Desires Bloom," by Pete Engardio, August 22, 2005, *Business Week* online extra. Available online at: http://www.businessweek.com/magazine/content/05_34/b3948531.htm

7. From "Report of Chinese Women Executives Situation Investigation," by the Guanghua School of Management at Beijing University, 2006. Only a Chinese version of the report is available online at: http://www.gsm.pku.edu.cn/store/object/200627204257report.pdf

8. From "Winning the Graduate Recruitment Battle in China," a presentation by the Corporate Leadership Council in association with Universum, September and October, 2006.

9. From "The 50 Most Powerful Women in Business: Global Power 50," October 16, 2006, *Fortune, 154,* pp. 190, 192. The 2006 international list is available online at: http://money.cnn.com/magazines/fortune/mostpowerfulwomen/2006/international/index.html

10. From "The 50 Most Powerful Women in Business: Global Power 50," November 14, 2005, *Fortune, 152,* pp. 157, 161, 163. The 2005 international list is available online at: http://money.cnn.com/magazines/fortune/mostpowerfulwomen/2005/international/

11. From "Divorce Rate Rises by 7%: Ministry," an article featured in *China Daily,* May 25, 2007. Available online at: http://www.chinadaily.com.cn/china/2007-05/25/content_880115.htm

Chapter 3

1. From "Winning the Graduate Recruitment Battle in China," a presentation by the Corporate Leadership Council in association with Universum, September and October, 2006.

2. Results posted on Procter & Gamble's web site on two web pages. The 2007 CLC survey results are available at http://www.pg.com.cn/job/news_01.asp; the ChinaHR.com results are available at http://www.pg.com.cn/job/news_04.asp.

3. From "Winning the Graduate Recruitment Battle in China."

4. Ibid.

Chapter 4

1. From *Leadership in China: Keeping Pace with a Growing Economy* (p. 14), by Paul R. Bernthal, Jason Bondra, and Wei Wang, 2005, Pittsburgh, PA: Development Dimensions International. Available through DDI's web site at: http://www.ddiworld.com/pdf/ddi_leadershipinchina_rr.pdf

2. From "China's Talent Wars," by Benjamin Robertson, March 2007, *Workforce Management Online.* Available online at: http://www.workforce.com/section/06/feature/24/78/95/index.html

3. Ibid.

4. To learn more about Development Dimensions International's interviewing system for selection and promotions, visit the Targeted Selection page on DDI's web site: http://www.ddiworld.com/products_services/targetedselection.asp

5. From the Law of the People's Republic of China on Employment Contracts, adopted at the 28th Session of the Standing Committee of the 10th National People's Congress on June 29, 2007. An unofficial English translation of the law is available online at: http://www.amcham-shanghai.org/NR/rdonlyres/DE724602-2608-4FF5-94E2-DDD2805521C3/4470/EmploymentContractLaw_BakerMcKenzie.pdf

6. From *Leadership in China,* Bernthal, Bondra, & Wang, pp. 14–15.

7. From "Chinese-Language Requirements Trips Up Goldman Executive," by Cathy Chan, July 13, 2007, *International Herald Tribune,* p. 12. Available online at: http://www.iht.com/articles/2007/07/12/bloomberg/bxgoldman.php

Chapter 5

1. Peter Drucker's quote featured in "From the Editors" in the *Leader to Leader Journal,* Winter 1997, p. 3. Available online at: http://www.drucker.org/knowledgecenter/journal.aspx?ArticleID=228

Chapter 6

1. Hewitt's ranking featured in "Spansion China," 2008, in *Hewitt Quarterly Asia Pacific, 5.* Available online at: http://www.hewittassociates.com/Intl/AP/en-AP/KnowledgeCenter/Magazine/HQ_18/articles/spansion-china.html

2. Palmisano quotation from "IBM Launches Major Services Initiative in China," an IBM press release, November 14, 2006. Available online at: http://www-03.ibm.com/press/us/en/pressrelease/20607.wss

3. Kleisterlee quotation from a speech published in the Philips publication *Challenges and Opportunities Created by China's Economic Growth,* November 2005, pp. 7, 3. Available online at: http://www.newscenter.philips.com/shared/assets/Downloadablefile/EFQM-2005-speech-Kleisterlee---final-15227.pdf

Chapter 8

1. From *Leadership in China: Keeping Pace with a Growing Economy* (pp. 5–8), by Paul R. Bernthal, Jason Bondra, and Wei Wang, 2005, Pittsburgh, PA: Development Dimensions International. Available through DDI's web site at: http://www.ddiworld.com/pdf/ddi_leadershipinchina_rr.pdf

2. Ibid., 8–11.

3. This *Hewitt Quarterly Asia Pacific* web page, "Asia's Best Employers Speak Out," features comments from Asia's top business leaders. Available online at: http://www.hewittassociates.com/Intl/AP/en-AP/KnowledgeCenter/Magazine/HQ_18/articles/asia-best-employers.html

4. From *Managing and Developing Talent in China and India* (p. 9), by Development Dimensions International, 2006, Pittsburgh, PA: Author.

Chapter 9

1. From *Leadership in China: Keeping Pace with a Growing Economy* (pp. 7, 11–12), by Paul R. Bernthal, Jason Bondra, and Wei Wang, 2005, Pittsburgh, PA: Development Dimensions International. Available through DDI's web site at: http://www.ddiworld.com/pdf/ddi_leadershipinchina_rr.pdf

Chapter 10

1. From the Law of the People's Republic of China on Employment Contracts, adopted at the 28th Session of the Standing Committee of the 10th National People's Congress on June 29, 2007. Also see "China's Contract Law: Something for Everyone," by Ed Frauenheim, 2007, *Workforce Management, 86,* pp. 35–39. Available online at: http://uwp.edu/~crooker/786-SHRM/articles/intl-china-wm-082007.pdf

Chapter 11

1. From "More Foreigners Working in China," an article in *Asia Pulse News,* June 1, 2007.

2. From "54,000 Foreigners Work in Shanghai," an article in *Chinanews,* May 11, 2007. An English blurb about the article is available online at: http://resources.madeinchina.com/b2b/resources,Bridge.shtml?newsid= 501221&type=3

3. Section taken from *Grow Your Own Leaders: How to Identify, Develop, and Retain Leadership Talent* (pp. 15–19, 50), by William C. Byham, Audrey B. Smith, and Matthew J. Paese, 2002, Upper Saddle River, NJ: Financial Times Prentice Hall.

4. See "Finding Future Perfect Senior Leaders: Spotting Executive Potential," by Robert W. Rogers and Audrey B. Smith, 2007, Pittsburgh, PA: Development Dimensions International. Available online through DDI's web site at: http://www.ddiworld.com/pdf/Finding_Future_Perfect_ar_ddi.pdf

DDI's Leadership Potential Factors were developed from research conducted by Morgan W. McCall, Jr. (see *Identifying Leadership Potential in Future International Executives: A Learning Resource Guide,* with Gretchen Spreitzer and Joan Mahoney, 1994); Brent W. Roberts and Robert Hogan (see *Personality Psychology in the Workplace,* 2001); Jim Collins (see "Level 5 Leadership" in *Harvard Business Review,* January 2001); and Ann Howard and Doug Bray (see "Predictions of Managerial Success Over Long Periods of Time: Lessons from the Management Progress Study," in *Measures of Leadership,* 1990).

5. From *Iacocca: An Autobiography* (p. 50), by Lee Iacocca and William Novak, 1984, New York: Bantam Books.

6. From *Factors Affecting the Acceptance and Application of Developmental Feedback from an Executive Assessment Program,* an unpublished doctoral dissertation by Tacy M. Byham, 2005, from the University of Akron. Available online at: http://www.ohiolink.edu/etd/view.cgi?akron1133214086

7. From "Winning the Graduate Recruitment Battle in China," a presentation by the Corporate Leadership Council in association with Universum, September and October, 2006.

8. From "Flight of Quality: With China's Economy Sizzling, Good Managers Are Scarce and Proving Ever Harder to Retain," by Lara Wozniak, 2003, *Far Eastern Economic Review, 166,* p. 101.

Chapter 12

1. From *Attracting and Retaining Critical Talent Segments (Volume III)* (p. 8), by the Corporate Leadership Council, 2006, Washington, DC: Corporate Executive Board.

2. From "Managing: Heart of the Matter—Why a Small Company in China Won the Top Spot in a Survey of Asia's Best Employers," by Cris Prystay, April 20, 2007, *The Wall Street Journal Asia,* p. W6. The text of the article also can be read online at: http://www.careerjournal.com/jobhunting/huntingabroad/20070424-prystay.html

3. From *Employee Retention in China 2007: The Flight of Human Talent* (p. 9), by Ann Howard, Louis Liu, Richard Wellins, and Steve Williams, 2007, Pittsburgh, PA: Development Dimensions International. Available online through DDI's web site at: http://www.ddiworld.com/pdf/ EmployeeRetentioninChina2007_ddi.pdf

4. Ibid., 10–12.

5. Ibid., 21.

6. Ibid., 23–24.

7. Ibid., 14.

8. From "Have You Got What It Takes?" an article featured in *Hewitt Quarterly Asia Pacific, 4,* May 2005. Available online at: http://www.hewittassociates. com/Intl/AP/en%2DAP/KnowledgeCenter/Magazine/HQ_13/articles/tittle2. html

9. Ibid.

Chapter 13

1. From "Culture Shock: A Fish Out of Water," by Elaine Addison, December 9, 2005, featured on the *World Corporater Culture* web site. Available online at: http://www.wccep.com/en/article/2005-12-9/131-1.htm

2. From *Inside Knowledge: Streetwise in Asia* (p. 13), by Michael Backman, 2005, New York: Palgrave Macmillan.

3. From *Your Chinese Roots: The Overseas Chinese Story* (chapter 12), by Thomas Tsu-Wee Tan, 1986, Singapore: Times Books International.

BIBLIOGRAPHY

Addison, E. (2005, December 9). Culture shock: A fish out of water. *World Corporater Culture.* Retrieved December 19, 2007, from http://www.wccep.com/en/article/2005-12-9/131-1.htm

Asia's best employers speak out. (2007). *Hewitt Quarterly Asia Pacific, 5*(2). Retrieved December 20, 2007, from http://www.hewittassociates.com/ Intl/AP/en-AP/KnowledgeCenter/Magazine/HQ_18/articles/ asia-best-employers.html

Backman, M. (2005). *Inside knowledge: Streetwise in Asia.* New York: Palgrave Macmillan.

Backman, M. (2007). *Asia future shock: Business crisis and opportunity in the coming years.* New York: Palgrave Macmillan.

Backman, M. (2007, March 28). China's counterfeit culture is quite an education. *The Age.*

Backman, M., & Butler, C. (2007). *Big in Asia: 30 strategies for business success* (Rev. ed.). New York: Palgrave Macmillan.

Bernthal, P.R., Bondra, J., & Wang, W. (2005). *Leadership in China: Keeping pace with a growing economy.* Pittsburgh, PA: Development Dimensions International. Available through DDI's web site at: http://www.ddiworld.com/pdf/ddi_leadershipinchina_rr.pdf

Bernthal, P.R., & Wellins, R.S. (2005). *China global comparison—Leadership forecast 2005–2006.* Pittsburgh, PA: Development Dimensions International. Available through DDI's web site at: http://www.ddiworld.com/pdf/ddi_leadershipforecast2005_report_cn.pdf

Bernthal, P.R., & Wellins, R.S. (2005). *Leadership forecast 2005–2006.* Pittsburgh, PA: Development Dimensions International.

Byham, T.M. (2005). *Factors affecting the acceptance and application of developmental feedback from an executive assessment program.* Unpublished doctoral dissertation, The University of Akron, Ohio.

Byham, W.C., Smith, A.B., & Paese, M.J. (2002). *Grow your own leaders: How to identify, develop, and retain leadership talent.* Upper Saddle River, NJ: Financial Times Prentice Hall.

Chan, C. (2007, July 13). Chinese-language requirements trips up Goldman executive. *International Herald Tribune,* p. 12.

Chaos in the classrooms. (2006, August 12). *The Economist, 380*(8490), 32–33.

China's people problem. (2005, April 16). *The Economist, 375*(8422), 53–54.

The Conference Board. (2007, October). *CEO challenge 2007: Top 10 challenges.* New York: Author.

Corporate Leadership Council. (2006). *Attracting and retaining critical talent segments (Volume III).* Washington, DC: Corporate Executive Board.

Corporate Leadership Council/Universum. (September/October, 2006). *Winning the graduate recruitment battle in China* [presentation].

Development Dimensions International. (2006). *Managing and developing talent in China and India.* Pittsburgh, PA: Author.

Divorce rate rises by 7%: Ministry. (2007, May 25). *China Daily.* Retrieved December 4, 2007, from http://www.chinadaily.com.cn/china/2007-05/25/content_880115.htm

Engardio, P. (2005, August 22). A thousand Chinese desires bloom. *Business Week* [online extra]. Retrieved December 4, 2007, from http://www.businessweek.com/magazine/content/05_34/b3948531.htm

Farrell, D., & Grant, A.J. (2005). China's looming talent shortage. *The McKinsey Quarterly,* (4), 70–79.

The 50 most powerful women in business: Global power 50. (2005, November 14). *Fortune, 152*(10), 157, 161, 163.

The 50 most powerful women in business: Global power 50. (2006, October 16). *Fortune, 154*(8), 190, 192.

54,000 foreigners work in Shanghai. (2007, May 11). *Chinanews.* Retrieved December 7, 2007, from http://www.chinanews.cn/news/2007-05-11/35771.html

Frauenheim, E. (2007, March 14). China's pay problems. Posted to *Workforce.com.* Retrieved from http://www.workforce.com/wpmu/globalwork/2007/03/14/china%E2%80%99s-pay-problems/

Frauenheim, E. (2007, August 20). China's contract law: Something for everyone. *Workforce Management, 86*(14), 35–39.

French, H.W. (2005, October 28). China strives for world-class universities. *International Herald Tribune,* section 3, p. 2.

From the editors. (1997, Winter). *Leader to Leader Journal,* (3), 2–3.

Grant, A., & Desvaux, G. (2005, May 18). Narrowing China's corporate leadership gap. *China Daily.* Retrieved from http://www.chinadaily.com.cn/english/doc/2005-05/18/content_443284.htm

Guanghua School of Management, Beijing University. (2006). *Report of Chinese women executives situation investigation.* Chinese version retrieved from http://www.gsm.pku.edu.cn/store/object/200627204257report.pdf

Harmsen, P. (2007, February 13). China suffers from worst brain drain in the world. *Agence France-Presse.* Retrieved from http://www.industryweek.com/ReadArticle.aspx?ArticleID=13604

Have you got what it takes? (2005, May). *Hewitt Quarterly Asia Pacific, 4*(1). Retrieved December 7, 2007, from http://www.hewittassociates.com/Intl/AP/en%2DAP/KnowledgeCenter/Magazine/HQ_13/articles/tittle2.html

Hewitt Associates. (2007, April 20). Hewitt announces best employers in China 2007 (press release). Retrieved December 17, 2007, from http://www.hewittassociates.com/Intl/AP/en-CN/AboutHewitt/Newsroom/PressReleases/2007/april-18-2007_a.aspx

Hewitt Consulting. (2007, September 17). *2007 Beijing city compensation and benefits study result presentation.* Conducted in Beijing City, China, using 2007 Hewitt China TCM study Beijing findings.

Howard, A., Liu, L., Wellins, R., & Williams, S. (2007). *Employee retention in China 2007: The flight of human talent.* Pittsburgh, PA: Development Dimensions International.

Iacocca, L., & Novak, W. (1984). *Iacocca: An autobiography.* New York: Bantam Books.

IBM. (2006, November 14). IBM launches major services initiative in China (press release). Retrieved from http://www-03.ibm.com/press/us/en/pressrelease/20607.wss

Kanellos, M. (2007, June 4). China's new weapon: Low executive pay. *ZDNET News.* San Francisco: CNET Networks. Retrieved from http://news.zdnet.com/2100-9595_22-6188306.html

Law of the People's Republic of China on employment contracts, adopted at the 28th session of the Standing Committee of the 10th National People's Congress on June 29, 2007. Unofficial English translation of the law prepared by Baker & McKenzie, Chicago. Available online at: http://www.amcham-shanghai.org/NR/rdonlyres/DE724602-2608-4FF5-94E2-DDD2805521C3/4470/EmploymentContractLaw_BakerMcKenzie.pdf

Lee, D. (2006, February 21). Job hopping is rampant as China's economy chases skilled workers. *Los Angeles Times,* p. C-1.

McDaniels, I. (2004, January). A critical eye on Shanghai: Will the city's extraordinary growth continue? *China Business Review.* Retrieved from http://www.chinabusinessreview.com/public/0401/shanghai_letter.html

Ministry of Education of People's Republic of China. *Number of students in regular HEIS by field of study.* Retrieved January 2008 from http://www.moe.edu.cn/edoas/website18/info33545.htm

More foreigners working in China. (2007, June 1). *Asia Pulse News.*

Philips. (2005, November). *Challenges and opportunities created by China's economic growth.* Philips Publications. Retrieved from http://www.newscenter.philips.com/shared/assets/Downloadablefile/EFQM-2005-speech-Kleisterlee---final-15227.pdf

Ping, Y. (2006, November 2). U.S. companies facing skills shortage. *China Daily.* Retrieved from http://en.bcnq.com/bizchina/2006-11/02/content_722530.htm

Procter & Gamble. (2007). P&G China No. 2 on "2006 best employer" ranking by ChinaHR.com, China's biggest online recruiter. Retrieved from http://www.pg.com.cn/job/news_04.asp

Procter & Gamble. (2007). P&G China No. 3 on "2007 ideal employer" ranking. Retrieved from http://www.pg.com.cn/job/news_01.asp

Prystay, C. (2007, April 20). Managing: Heart of the matter—Why a small company in China won the top spot in a survey of Asia's best employers. *The Wall Street Journal Asia,* p. W6.

Roberts, D. (2006, December 4). China MBAs: Most likely to fall short. *Business Week,* (4012), 106–107. Retrieved from http://www.businessweek.com/magazine/content/06_49/b4012094.htm

Robertson, B. (2007, March). China's talent wars. *Workforce Management Online.* Retrieved November 28, 2007, from http://www.workforce.com/section/06/feature/24/78/95/index.html

Rogers, R.W., & Smith, A.B. (2007). *Finding future perfect senior leaders: Spotting executive potential* (white paper). Pittsburgh, PA: Development Dimensions International. Available online through DDI's web site at: http://www.ddiworld.com/pdf/Finding_Future_Perfect_ar_ddi.pdf

Salary growth: What you earn. (2007, March 31). *The Economist, 382*(8522), 113. Retrieved from http://www.economist.com/daily/chartgallery/displaystory.cfm?story_id=8909327

Shakers: ABB planning to use cash for acquisitions (a China bank chief lags behind in pay). (2006, May 11). *International Herald Tribune.* Retrieved from http://www.iht.com/articles/2006/05/10/bloomberg/bxshake.php

Spansion China. (2007). *Hewitt Quarterly Asia Pacific, 5*(2). Retrieved from http://www.hewittassociates.com/Intl/AP/en-AP/KnowledgeCenter/Magazine/HQ_18/articles/spansion-china.html

Tan, R., & Wellins, R. (2006, November). Growing today's Chinese leaders for tomorrow's needs: Developing business leaders could make or break China's economic growth. "India & China Inc." supplement to *T+D, 60,* 20–23. Retrieved from http://www.ddiworld.com/pdf/td_novci_supplement.pdf

Tan, T.T. (1986). *Your Chinese roots: The overseas Chinese story.* Singapore: Times Books International.

Thornton, J.L. (2006, March 15). China's next generation: Perspectives on future leaders. Speech featured in *S.C. Fan Memorial Lecture,* The University of Hong Kong.

Tripathi, S. (2006, January 5). India's skill shortage. *The Wall Street Journal Asia,* p. 13.

U.S. Census Bureau's International Data Base. (2007). Population pyramids for China—2007. Retrieved from http://www.census.gov/cgibin/ipc/idbpyry.pl?cty=CH&maxp=67043344&maxa=100&ymax=300&yr=2007&.submit=Submit+Query

Wozniak, L. (2003, December 25). Flight of quality: With China's economy sizzling, good managers are scarce and proving ever harder to retain. *Far Eastern Economic Review, 166*(51), 101.

Xinhua News Agency. (2007, March 7). More than half of Chinese can speak Mandarin. *China View.* Retrieved November 28, 2007, from http://news.xinhuanet.com/english/2007-03/07/content_5812838.htm

ACKNOWLEDGMENTS

Just as writing this book required a team effort of the authors' working across a dozen time zones, so too did bringing it from draft, to manuscript, to the final edited, formatted version. Along the way many associates, friends, and colleagues contributed in many different ways. We, the authors, deeply appreciate their efforts and wish to recognize them here. They include:

Michael Backman, who helped us take the book from idea to manuscript. He specializes in Asia's economies and corporate practices, and he lent his considerable expertise to our effort. Michael authored the international best seller *Asian Eclipse: Exposing the Dark Side of Business in Asia* (John Wiley & Sons, 1999), named by *The Economist* magazine as one of the 16 finest nonfiction books published for the year. He has authored or coauthored five other books on Asian business and culture and has a long-running, widely read Asian business column in Melbourne's *The Age* newspaper. He has lived and worked in Asia and is a frequent speaker at conferences and seminars on the topic of Asia, both for companies and at public events. When not traveling in Asia, he lives in London. Michael's knowledge of Asia and its business world was absolutely crucial in writing this book.

Helen Wylie, who coordinated the authors' efforts, documented revisions, set up phone meetings, and generally kept everyone up to date from the book's "idea" phase through its nine iterations. This often meant working across various time zones at any given time, on any given day of the week. Helen also had the dubious task of transcribing at least one author's barely legible, handwritten revisions and typing them accurately into the manuscript. She was there when we needed to locate source material, and she helped to coordinate the efforts of our research associate. Helen's considerable planning and organizing skills were sorely tested on several occasions, yet she came through each time in exemplary fashion. Helen is a veteran of several book productions now, including *Grow Your Own Leaders* (FT Press, 2002) and *70: The New 50* (DDI Press, 2007) and, as with those works, we could not have succeeded without her.

Bill Proudfoot—managing editor—joined the team somewhere around the third draft and worked through another six iterations. As he did with *Grow Your Own Leaders* and *70: The New 50,* Bill put in a considerable number of hours editing, proofing, and polishing drafts before managing the final version through formatting and final proofing and into our print shop. Thanks to Bill, the book production met our deadline. His extensive experience working on previous DDI books and other DDI products paid dividends as he navigated interim deadlines, kept production on track, worked with multiple authors to incorporate their individual and collective revisions, and ensured that the prose delivered a consistent tone and message. On more than one occasion, Bill checked our intent by asking, "Is this what we really want to say here?" Saying *thanks* can't begin to express our appreciation for the work that Bill did.

Janet Wiard, our graphic design wizard, was another major player in the production of this book. Janet designed the crisp, clean format and graphics, and it was her idea to incorporate the Chinese characters into the design. Another veteran of DDI book design and production, Janet, who is an expert with the formatting software, typeset the entire volume from a series of text files and persevered through numerous last-minute revisions. Her attention to detail in revising the text and graphics was outstanding. Excellent work, Janet!

As he has on previous DDI book productions, **Shawn Garry** once again wore many hats during this project: proofreader, second editor, reference checker, and "the audience." Shawn joined the team late in the manuscript process to lend his editorial eye to editing and proofing the text before it was typeset. Then, once the book had been formatted, he proofed it again. Shawn also worked closely with our research associate to verify the dozens of references that appear in the End Notes section. Last, but not least, he compiled the comprehensive bibliography and assisted with the index. Great job, Shawn!

DDI research on leadership and selection practices in China underpins much of this book. We want to thank **Paul Bernthal, Ann Howard, Evan Sinar,** and **Rich Wellins** for their significant contributions in obtaining this meaningful data about China and its employees and then interpreting it.

We also acknowledge the contributions of **Carla Fogle,** who served as our research associate; **Susan Ryan,** who designed the cover; **Patrice Andres,** who helped with graphics; **Tammy Pordash,** who spent many hours transcribing authors' dictation; **Colby Fazio,** who has been working to market the book; and **Jennifer Pesci-Kelly,** our public relations liaison.

Other associates and colleagues volunteered their time to review earlier versions of this book. Their feedback was of immense help in improving the content of *Leadership Success in China: An Expatriate's Guide.* Reviewers included **P.H. Chang, Margaret Cheng, Timothy Collier, Bruce Court, Ann Howard, Kenzie Kwong,** and **Bob Rogers.**

Thanks, too, to **Wallance Ma, Ron Norris, Linda Talley,** and **Linda Wan** for their constructive support throughout the process.

ABOUT DDI

Since 1970 Development Dimensions International (DDI) has helped some of the world's most successful organizations achieve superior business results by building engaged, high-performing workforces.

We excel in two major areas: designing and implementing selection systems that enable our partner organizations to hire better people faster; and identifying and developing exceptional leadership talent crucial to creating a workforce that drives sustainable success.

Our key differentiator is *realization*—we focus on the outcomes our clients need and feel a passion for their success. Our 1,000 associates, located in 76 offices and 26 countries, work with individual clients to craft and implement solutions that truly improve performance.

For more information about DDI's programs and services or to learn more about our client experiences, visit our web site at **www.ddiworld.com**.

About DDI Asia

DDI's network of Asian offices has been supporting both multinational and local corporations in Greater China since 1990. DDI Asia currently has more than 80 associates serving clients from four major Chinese cities: Beijing, Hong Kong, Shanghai, and Taipei. We also have offices in Singapore, Kuala Lumpur, and Bangkok.

In addition, partner organizations in Japan, Korea, Indonesia, and the Philippines provide a wide spectrum of capabilities to our clients through more than 300 DDI-certified consultants, trainers, and assessors.

Most of our products and services are available in multiple languages, such as Mandarin, Cantonese, Japanese, Bahasa, Indonesian, Thai, Korean, Bahasa Melayu, and Tagalog.

ABOUT THE AUTHORS

The authors bring widely divergent experience to this book. Each has a unique perspective on the expatriate experience in China.

Yue-er Luo, D.B.A.

Dr. Luo has 25 years' experience in both the consulting and corporate environments in Greater China.

Her first period of experience in mainland China started in 1989 with Development Dimensions International (DDI), based in Hong Kong as the marketing director for DDI Asia-Pacific. In that position until 1996, she was one of DDI's pioneers in helping clients adapt their selection and leadership assessment system and leadership development training for the China culture. The clients she consulted with included Motorola, Nortel, SC Johnson, Johnson & Johnson, United Technology, Chengdu Aerotech, Pfizer, and Shangri-La Hotels.

From 2002 to 2005, Dr. Luo was back in Shanghai on the start-up team for Taiwan Semiconductor Manufacturing Company Ltd. Working with a local team, she created and set up the HR systems to recruit, train, and develop the first 800 employees for the company's Shanghai operation.

Dr. Luo currently teaches a strategic human resources program in the EMBA program of Cheung Kong Graduate School of Business (Beijing). She also is a visiting professor at the Hong Kong University of Science and Technology.

Teaching at these business schools, Dr. Luo leverages her HR insights while educating China's CEOs and senior executives.

Dr. Luo's consulting experience makes her one of the unique veteran experts with both the strategic and operational experience to address such hot China human resource issues as talent development, retention, and performance management.

Erik Duerring

Erik Duerring is an American expatriate in China. He spends a great deal of time with both expatriate and local senior managers consulting on selection, executive assessment, coaching, and development programs.

Mr. Duerring, DDI's director of consulting services in Asia, has more than 12 years' experience in succession management, assessment, and leadership development, covering a variety of industries. Across eight locations he is responsible for formulating and executing DDI Asia's consulting strategies through a team of consultants, executive coaches, project managers, trainers, instructional designers, and support resources.

Since 2002 he has worked with DDI's Asia operations, offering project management, consulting, and sales support. In 2006 he launched mainland China's first executive assessment center. In 2007 Mr. Duerring was honored by HRoot and *World Management Review* magazine as a winner of the prestigious 50 People of Human Resources in China award. The award recognizes those entrepreneurs, experts, and scholars who make remarkable contributions to and stimulate the development of the human resource industry in China.

Mr. Duerring is frequently interviewed and quoted in the mainland China and Asia news media as an expert on talent management. Throughout China and Asia he has spoken at numerous public conferences and MNC senior leadership forums on the strategic selection, assessment, and development of human talent.

William Byham, Ph.D.

Dr. Byham is cofounder, chairman, and CEO of Development Dimensions International.

A frequent traveler to China, Dr. Byham contributed his insights from the perspective of DDI's global research into selection and leadership practices and DDI's interviews with more than 40 CEOs in China as part of CNBC's Asian Business Leaders Award (ABLA).

Dr. Byham also leveraged his own experiences leading an international organization and his years of personal experience helping organizations throughout the world realize their productivity, quality, and retention goals.

Over the last four decades, Dr. Byham has pioneered a number of important human resource technologies and systems that have had a significant impact on organizations throughout the world. These technologies include the assessment center method, behavior-based interviewing (Targeted Selection®), behavioral job analysis methodology, results-based employee and management training and development (Interaction Management®), empowerment, retirement management, and the use of the Acceleration Pool® as a method of succession management for high-potential individuals. These technologies have been described in the 23 books and more than 200 articles and monographs he has either authored or coauthored.

The DDI China Team

Many of this book's insights into the challenges that expatriate managers face in China came from consulting and executive coaching done by DDI's teams of Chinese nationals.

DDI's network of Asian offices has been supporting both multinational and local corporations in Greater China since 1990.

In the Greater China region, we currently have more than 80 associates serving clients from four major cities: Beijing, Hong Kong, Shanghai, and Taipei.

Our China associates have been recognized for their efforts in providing best practices through research, localized products, and solutions with state-of-the-art technologies. For example, DDI China was honored by HRoot and *World Management Review* with the "Best Assessment Organization in Greater China" award as part of their 2006–2007 Annual HR Awards. This was DDI China's third assessment award. In 2005 Asia Pacific Human Resource Research Association named DDI China the "Outstanding Talent Assessment Consulting Organization." The China Annual Human Resources Award Ceremony and *World Management Review* named DDI "Best Human Resources Assessment Brand 2006." In addition, DDI China was honored by HRoot with the "Best HR Consultant Organization in China" award in 2006.

OTHER BOOKS FROM DDI

Empowered Teams: Creating Self-Directed Work Groups That Improve Quality, Productivity, and Participation by Richard S. Wellins, William C. Byham, and Jeanne M. Wilson

Grow Your Own Leaders by William C. Byham, Audrey B. Smith, and Matthew J. Paese

HeroZ™—Empower Yourself, Your Coworkers, Your Company by William C. Byham and Jeff Cox (available in English, French, German, Spanish, Korean, Chinese, Arabic, and Portuguese)

Inside Teams: How 20 World-Class Organizations Are Winning Through Teamwork by Richard S. Wellins, William C. Byham, and George R. Dixon

Landing the Job You Want: How to Have the Best Job Interview of Your Life by William C. Byham with Debra Pickett

Leadership Trapeze: Strategies for Leadership in Team-Based Organizations by Jeanne M. Wilson, Jill George, and Richard S. Wellins, with William C. Byham

Organizational Change That Works: How to Merge Culture and Business Strategies for Maximum Results by Robert W. Rogers, John W. Hayden, and B. Jean Ferketish, with Robert Matzen

Realizing the Promise of Performance Management by Robert W. Rogers

The Selection Solution: Solving the Mystery of Matching People to Jobs by William C. Byham with Steven M. Krauzer

The Service Leaders Club by William C. Byham with Ray Crew and James H.S. Davis

70: The New 50 by William C. Byham

Shogun Management™: How North Americans Can Thrive in Japanese Companies by William C. Byham with George Dixon

Succeeding With Teams: 101 Tips That Really Work by Richard S. Wellins, Dick Schaaf, and Kathy Harper Shomo

Team Leader's Survival Guide by Jeanne M. Wilson and Jill A. George

Team Member's Survival Guide by Jill A. George and Jeanne M. Wilson

Zapp!® Empowerment in Health Care by William C. Byham with Jeff Cox and Greg Nelson

Zapp!® in Education by William C. Byham with Jeff Cox and Kathy Harper Shomo

Zapp!® The Lightning of Empowerment—revised edition by William C. Byham with Jeff Cox (original edition available in English, French, German, Japanese, Dutch, Chinese, Korean, Portuguese, and Spanish)

GLOSSARY OF CHINESE TERMS USED IN THIS BOOK

guanxi   a person's business network, contacts, or connections; the loyalty a direct report shows his or her leader; the desire to achieve harmony between individuals and organizations

guo qing   how things are done in China

hong bao   a red envelope with money in it, often distributed during festivals such as Chinese New Year; the packets often are decorated with lucky symbols that represent luck and wealth; gift of cash (i.e., when somebody asks for *hong bao* in a business situation, the person is asking for a monetary gift)

hukou   a residential permit for a specific city that entitles the holder to certain residential rights (e.g., an education allowance for the children attending its public schools)

laowai   foreigners to China

xiaojies   bar hostesses

INDEX

A

Acceleration Center (DDI), 66, 159, 170
  day in the life of a participant, 67–68, 160
  defined, 66
  development opportunities, 66
  example, 170
  as high-level assessment centers, 66

Acceleration Pool (DDI), 153, 154–157, 186
  building an, 154–157
  compared to retention planning, 154–155
  defined, 154
  example, 170
  featured in *Grow Your Own Leaders,* 154–157
  aka high-potential or high-flyer pools, 154
  identifying high potentials for an, 157–160
  in a large company, 156
  and leadership pipelines, 153–161
  in a midsize company, 155
  in several business units, 156–157
  size of, 156

accountability, 134–135
  difficult for Chinese to understand, 134–135
  example scenarios, 135

agreement, creating, 90–93

American Chamber of Commerce (Shanghai), 6

Asimco Technologies, 167

assessment centers, 38, 52, 56, 57, 63, 65–66
  Acceleration Center, 66
  development plans, 65–66
  as larger-scale simulations, 65
  used to supplement interview data, 65–66

assessment selection process, 56, 57

assignments/rotations for high potentials, 167–168

attracting qualified applicants, 31–44, 57
  branding your company, 31–33
  most sought-after companies, 32–33
  mounting an all-out recruiting campaign, 41–44
  offering learning opportunities, 32, 33, 36, 40, 43
  preferred employer nationalities, 34
  preferred job sectors, 34
  role of *hukou* in, 37, 38
  selection process, 56, 57
  strategies, 43–44
  top brands in China, 31–33
  university campaigns and visits, 39–40